MY UNCLE SAM

I0139750

Len Jenkin

BROADWAY PLAY PUBLISHING INC
224 E 62nd St, NY, NY 10065
www.broadwayplaypub.com
info@broadwayplaypub.com

First printing, this edition: June 2015
I S B N: 978-0-88145-619-6

Book design: Marie Donovan
Page make-up: Adobe InDesign
Typeface: Palatino
Printed and bound in the U S A

MY UNCLE SAM was first presented by the New York Shakespeare Festival Public Theater on 7 October 1983. The cast was as follows:

DARLENE/LITTLE PERSON ....Laura Innes
THE BOTTLER... Olek Krupa
LILA.. Kathleen Layman
OLD SAM .... Mark Margolis
JAKE/PROF FINLEY/GOLF MANAGER ....John Nesci
SACRISTAN/ASST TRAVEL AGENT .... Kristine Nielsen
CAPABILITY BROWN/MEXICAN DOCTOR ....Rocco Sisto
AUTHOR/TRAVEL AGENT........................Scott Wentworth
MISS SIMMONS/STELLA ....Margaret Whitton
YOUNG SAM .... R Hamilton Wright
MR FLEAGLE/LIGHTHOUSE KEEPER .... Ray Xifo

Director ....Len Jenkin
Set design ....John Arnone
Lighting design ....Frances Aronson
Costume design .... Kurt Wilhelm
Sound design ....Len Jenkin
Stage manager ....Jane Hubbard
Choreography .... Catlin Cobb

PRODUCTION NOTE

The Narrators should not be consistent reappearing characters. They are always different, and often visually conform to the setting in which they appear (nautical in Lighthouse etc). They can be actors who play other roles, in or out of character. They can appear briefly to say their lines, or be present longer during the scene, or even be offstage on mike—this to depend on the style and requirements of each individual production.

ACT ONE

1

(The AUTHOR, *alone. In another area, a nightclub* DUO *[man and woman]. They are lip-synching badly to a record, with exaggerated romantic gestures. An elderly man in a suit and tie listens to them.)*

DUO.
This is my story, I have no song
But a lone and broken heart—
Because I fell in love, in love with you—
I pray that you'll come back to me
Just to hear you say you love me, and we'll never never part
Never never part—oooh oooooh, oooh oooh —

(They fade, as the figure of My Uncle Sam, the elderly listener, rises. He is as described by the AUTHOR. *He stands quietly.)*

AUTHOR: I saw my Uncle Sam once a year. He was my grandfather's brother, my great-Uncle Sam actually. He was exotic. Points of exoticism: ONE: he lived in Pittsburgh, which may not be exotic if you're from Pittsburgh, but if you're seven years old and have never been anywhere, and don't know anybody who's ever been anywhere, Pittsburgh means a complete other place, with its own other kind of people and cars and houses which I could only imagine at the very edges of my consciousness...a parallel world full of

stuff made up in your head, and Uncle Sam would
walk through the door with the smell of Pittsburgh
in his thinning hair—dust of that impossible place on
his shoulders. Point of Exoticism TWO: he lived in a
hotel. I had never even seen a hotel, except in a movie,
where a hotel was a place only for adults, featuring
sex and adventure. THREE: he was a bachelor. I knew
that meant he wasn't married, but that special name
for it, and the way it was said about him, was a label
I couldn't read. I knew it meant he lived some other
way from us—different, and not quite respectable.
FOUR: He had a moustache, which he waxed. FIVE:
He wore expensive cashmere coats. SIX: He smoked
cigars. *(The figure lights a cigar.)* The simple truth,
which I can now understand as I am no longer seven,
is that my great Uncle Sam was a travelling salesman
in Pennsylvania. I understand bachelor and hotel and
Pittsburgh very well. I've even been there, and yet a
certain mystery never leaves his image in my mind.
He would give me five dollar bills. That was so much
money I never knew what to do with it but hide it. He
gave me a Viewmaster, with circles of Asia, and Peru,
and the U.S.A. I can almost dismiss it—pretend I can
understand him without that sense of strangeness I
always felt in his presence…but now I know that My
Uncle Sam stepped aside, in some extraordinary way,
from everything around him, and made that stepping
aside his life. He died alone. When he died he left me
all the money he had. Four hundred and ten dollars. I
hadn't seen him for thirty years. When I was little he
never told me a story. I'm telling myself one, for him.
Now. UNCLE SAM SOLD NOVELTIES!!

(The company, as SALESMEN, *including the* AUTHOR, MY
UNCLE SAM, *and a young man with a moustache who we
will discover to be* MY UNCLE SAM *in his youth.* OLD *and*
YOUNG SAM *speak together at times. They are linked by*

similarities in costume. All are in the postures of forties salesmen. The SALESMEN *take these lines by turn, and demonstrate as they speak. One has a Viewmaster.)*

SALESMEN: French batmask, pert and saucy! There's a certain spice to this style.
Ubangi lady and gentleman masks, hundred percent rubber!
Religious items! The luminous crucifix.
Jumbo chicken feet! Yellow molded plastic!
Hairy gorilla feet! Genuine black rubber, imbedded with black plastic hair!

OLD SAM: Unusual costume accessories: jungle drums boudoir set, a daringly designed two-piecer, inspired by darkest Africa, with frou-frou fringe!

ALL: OOOOOH!

OLD SAM: Leaves barely enough to the imagination to be legal.

ALL: OOOOOH!

SALESMEN: Genuine imitation platinum French ring with views. Bathing beauties! The Panama Canal.

OLD SAM: You say you want more for your money?

YOUNG SAM: You say what you've already heard just ain't enough? Tell you what I'm gonna do. Devil tail! Old Switch himself would be proud to wear this three foot long beauty!

ALL: OOOOOH!

YOUNG SAM: Frenchman kit!

SALESMEN: Beret, moustache, beard, cigarette holder!

ALL: OOOOOH!

AUTHOR: Chinky Chinaman kit: a genuine thinking cap, a pair of foo-yong goggles with slit eyes, a pair of special protruding plastic teeth.

YOUNG SAM: Pussy-cat kit. Purrfecti. Wear with a
black bikini. Plush cat ears, pom-pom cattail, jumbo
eyelashes, black gloves!

ALL: Ooooohh!

OLD SAM: Goozelum Goggles!

ALL: Ooooohh!

YOUNG SAM: The poo-poo cushion!

ALL: OOOH!

OLD SAM: The joy buzzer!

ALL: OOOOOOHH!

YOUNG SAM: The x-ray specs!

ALL: OOOOH!

OLD SAM: I AM MY UNCLE SAM. Next time you meet
me, you're gonna thank me.

(The group gathers around OLD SAM *curiously. A* MAN
narrates.)

MAN: *(As others listen attentively.)* After a certain period
in his life, he contrived, or rather he…happened…to
sever himself from the world—to vanish—

ALL: Aaaah!

MAN: —to give up his place and privileges with living
men, without being admitted among the dead.

(They slowly back away, staring at OLD SAM. YOUNG
SAM *is the last to leave. They're gone. Three* SECRETARIES
remain, in a row, pencils poised.)

OLD SAM: I am My Uncle Sam.

*(*OLD SAM *settles in to speak. He is in his hotel room in
Pittsburgh. Old armchair. Standing ashtray. The three
SECRETARIES cross their legs. When he speaks they start
writing, taking dictation. He does not notice them.)*

OLD SAM: I am a bachelor. I live in this hotel. Sherman
Arms, Pittsburgh. I came into this world seventy years
ago without a dime, and I've about held my own to
date. I'm not feeling well. I'm home from work today.
Called in sick, but they know there's no action on
my route this time of year. Allentown across to East
Stroudsburg. So I'm here at my window—and out
there, the Monongahela, as usual, Jones and Laughlin
steel on the river, plumes of fire off the stacks. My stars
at night. See 'em from my window. Sherman Arms.
Not night yet, but I'm waiting. I like the dusk. I like to
watch the lights go on in people's apartment windows
in the evening. And off, late at night. The only times
you're really certain somebody's there. I'm sitting in
Market Square yesterday, and this young guy with
a Pirates cap on sits next to me and opens his lunch.
Peanut butter. I'm thinking his mommy made it for
him now that's sweet, and then this gorgeous blonde
who's all of eighteen comes toward us and I'm thinking whatever you want darlin' it's eight to five I'll do it.
She's getting closer, and I'm watching every move. She
waltzes up and sits down on the kid's lap, like I'm not
there. They walk away, holding hands. And I'm full
of envy for him up to the top of my head and beyond.
And then I see them together in ten years screaming at
each other in the kitchen, and he picks up a wine glass
and throws it through a window and I remember that
it's not envy that's for the living. It's pity. Envy is for
the dead. I'm too smart to keep thinking that young
girls ask me for directions downtown cause they think
I'm an interesting guy, moustache and all, like I'm
somebody in a movie—like I'm a character…I am no
longer more interesting to good looking young women,
than a lamp post…I love secretaries…

(SECRETARIES *cross legs, continue taking his "dictation".)*

OLD SAM: I am no longer more interesting to Pittsburgh secretarial talent than a well.

SECRETARY 1: *(To* SECRETARY 2*)* A well?

SECRETARY 2. Well.

OLD SAM: Now let's say you're in Pittsburgh. A tourist in Market Square. Center of the universe. You're lost. Transparent as I am, you spot me, like seeing a shadow. I am quasi-neutered by age. I am unlikely to stab you or rape you, so if you want neither of those things to happen to you on this gray morning I am a good person to ask directions. I'm moving slow. You catch up to me. I'm not busy.... Tell you what I know. Listen. You got time... What's your life anyway? A few winters waiting for spring. A few summers waiting for the first clean chill of fall. A few bottles of whiskey, and three or four women you remember—if you're lucky. You might as well die now as later. Dust to dust, a fine darkness drifting with the dust of every other thing into a perpetual night. Even the names are dust. Names of the dead ... last to go. Just as well. We got a way out of this world that's wide open.

(The AUTHOR *appears behind the* SECRETARIES.*)*

OLD SAM: Directions. I know Pittsburgh perfect. Purrfect. I used to sell punchboards on the south side. Drugstores. Candy stores. I drove every turn of those streets in a Buick Roadmaster.

SECRETARY 1: A what?

SECRETARY 2: It's a car.

OLD SAM: However, it is possible my information is no longer current. I could tell you how to get out to Medvink's Drugs on Howland, told the desk man to head out there to buy his granddaughter something for her birthday. He came up here. Only time he ever did that. Opened my damn door with his key. He yells-

DESKMAN: *(V O)* NO SUCH PLACE!

OLD SAM: No such place. I had directed him to 1948...I missed something back there. My own damn fault. Been looking ever since, but you get so you know you won't find it. Hell, you don't even know what it was, passed by so quick— but you keep looking out of habit—or else you'd have to say, well, what I am now, what I'm doing now, this is my life. What man wants to say that? 1948. I had a girlfriend then...

SECRETARIES. Oooooh!

AUTHOR: That's enough. Got it?

SECRETARIES. We got it!

(The AUTHOR *and* SECRETARIES *exit,* OLD SAM *looks after retreating secretaries, winks at audience.)*

OLD SAM: Rowff! I was quite the sheik in my youth. First in town to have a luminous hatband... Had just started travelling for Apex Novelties...

*(*YOUNG SAM *appears in the distance. He's sharp; nervous, full of energy, carrying a suitcase.* OLD SAM *gestures toward him, then toward himself.* YOUNG SAM *is gone.)*

OLD SAM: I had a girlfriend then. Did I say that? We were engaged. Her name was Lila... She worked in a club here in town. She was a hostess.

*(*LILA *appears. The Nightclub. The same two entertainers as at the opening singing a song, exaggerated romantic gestures.* OLD SAM *and* YOUNG SAM *are gone.)*

SINGERS: *(Lip syncing)*
Cross over the bridge, cross over the bridge
Change your reckless way of living, cross over the
   bridge
Leave your fickle past behind you, and true romance
   will find you
Sister— Cross over the bridge.

(JAKE, *a tough looking man, drinks at a table alone. Other customers. The* M C *steps into the spotlight…*)

2

M C: Good evening to all you wonderful people here in the Club dez Morts. That's French for parlez-vous and how are you. You don't have to nudge her, sir. I think she got that one. Either you're all sleeping and I'm awake—or vice-versa. Hey—you be in my dreams, I'll be in yours. Love it. You know, these moments before the show where I get to be in close personal touch with all you wonderful people—hey, it's my life. What can I say? You're beautiful, each and every one of you, and it's beautiful that you're here with us tonight. No lie. Heart to heart. This story about My Uncle Sam is really something special. It can give you a lift—if you get me. Cure your warts. Heal cancer of the blood, save your marriage and ease your mind. When you go home tonight, tell it to your children. Whisper it in their ears while they sleep, like a brand new dream .

WOMAN: *(At table)* Get off!

M C: Before we begin, I want to say hello to a very special someone—met her only last night down at the Trailways Terminal, and tonight, she's with us in the audience.

WOMAN: Get off!

M C: Hey—I want you to take this performance as my gift—personally—you know who you are.

WOMAN: GET THE HELL OFF.

M C: *(Retreating offstage.)* Heart to heart to heart to heart…

(The singing duo takes the stage, continuing their song as before. LILA *crosses to* JAKE.*)*

DUO:
If you've built a boat to take you to the greener side
And if you've built that boat of every lie you've ever
    lied
You'll never reach the promised land of love I
    guarantee
For lies can not hold water and you'll sink into the sea.
Cross over the bridge...

(Over the song, the WOMAN *at the table narrates:)*

WOMAN: A nightclub in Pittsburgh. A man and a
woman *(She gestures toward* JAKE *and* LILA.*)* at a corner
table. He wears a loud sport jacket. She wears a black
taffeta evening dress. He drinks beer. She sips a pink
lady.

LILA: The least you could do, since we're engaged, you
come to my place of employment, you could look like
something.

JAKE: Whattaya want me to look like?

LILA: Something. You could wear a tie, at least. Where
do you think you are? The turkish bath? This is a
nightclub.

JAKE: Drink your pink lady, Lila.

LILA: I've never been so humiliated.

JAKE: I'm warning you, baby.

LILA: I do nothing but brag about you around here,
Jake. I tell everyone you're gonna find my brother
for me, and then we're gonna get married—and you
come in looking like something they dragged outta the
Monongahela river. When are you leaving?

JAKE: First thing in the morning.

LILA: You remember everything I told you?

JAKE: Yeah.

LILA: All the people?

JAKE: Yeah.

LILA: You know how to get to the light?

JAKE: Yeah.

LILA: Find him, Jake. He owes me. Daddy left us both that dough from the Tunnel Job. Fifty-fifty. Only I was a kid, so he tells my brother where he stashes it. Then Daddy is sitting in the Teepee Tavern drinking an Iron City, when his partner in the job shows up and asks a question. Where's the money? Daddy was reticent. His partner put an ice pick through his chest. Three days later my brother disappeared.

JAKE: Who was the partner?

LILA: You ever hear of the Bottler?

(A cop, plainclothes, enters.)

JAKE: Shut up!

LILA: What . .

JAKE: Shut up and reach under the table. I'm handing you a gun. Grab it.

LILA: Whatsa matter?

JAKE: Grab the heater, willya. A cop I know just walked in.

LILA: What am I gonna do with it?

JAKE: I don't care what you do with it. Sit on it.

LILA: O K, Jake. O K.

JAKE: Make some conversation. He spotted me.

LILA: They make pink ladies with gin. Gin and something red…

NARRATOR: Meanwhile, on his way to visit Lila at the club, Sam stops in at the Chinese laundry to see if his shirts ate ready.

(In another area, YOUNG SAM *appears fumbling in his pocket in front of a wire cage, Chinese letters above.)*

Uh-oh! He lost his ticket.

LAUNDRYMAN: No tickee, no washee.

(This scene fades as we return to the nightclub—)

PLAINCLOTHES MAN: Hello Jake. Out for a good time?

JAKE: It just got ruined.

LILA: Well, if you gentlemen'll excuse me... *(She walks off, concealing the gun .)*

PLAINCLOTHES MAN: Cute kid.

JAKE: Yeah. Class.

PLAINCLOTHES MAN: Stand up Jake. I said, stand up. Let's see what you got on you.

*(*PLAINCLOTHES MAN *frisks* JAKE.*)*

JAKE: I'm clean.

PLAINCLOTHES MAN: Jake, I come in here now and then, and I don't want my digestion getting upset by seeing your face.

JAKE: I'm leaving town in the morning.

PLAINCLOTHES MAN: Not soon enough. Get outta here—now. Move.

(As JAKE *exits he passes* LILA.*)*

LILA: *(To* JAKE.*)* See ya, big boy. Get your man, get his money, and get out.

JAKE: So long, Lila. Keep it warm for me, hah. *(To* PLAINCLOTHES MAN, *pointing at* LILA.*)* Like I said, class.

PLAINCLOTHES MAN: Yeah. One in a million. Move.

*(*JAKE *takes a step toward exit, freezes.)*

NARRATOR 1: Jake's going off to find Lila's brother.

*(*JAKE *exits.)*

NARRATOR 1: If he finds him, and gets the money, Lila says she'll marry Jake. I think Lila tells the same story to all the boys...

(YOUNG SAM *enters.*)

YOUNG SAM: Lila!

(LILA *and* YOUNG SAM *embrace, move to the same table* LILA *sat at with* JAKE.)

NARRATOR 1: In a few moments, Lila and Sam are deep in conversation...

LILA: In Port Desire, a gentleman with a bright light—

YOUNG SAM: A bright light.

NARRATOR 2: *(To audience.)* In Port Desire, a gentleman with a bright light—

LILA: A gentleman who is a teacher—

YOUNG SAM: A teacher—

NARRATOR 2: A gentleman who is a teacher.

NARRATOR 1: Now Lila's telling Sam she'll marry him if he finds her brother.

LILA: I'll marry you if you find my brother.

NARRATOR 1: She's listing some people who might have some information about his whereabouts...

LILA: A gentleman with a big book—

YOUNG SAM: A big book—

NARRATOR 2: A gentleman with a big book.

LILA: A lady in a golden vest—

YOUNG SAM: A golden vest—

NARRATOR 2: A lady in a golden vest.

LILA: A man with eight flags—

YOUNG SAM: Eight flags—

NARRATOR 2: A man with eight flags.

LILA: A lady in a violet gown—

YOUNG SAM: Violet gown—

NARRATOR 2: A lady in a violet gown.

LILA: A gentleman who is a gardener

YOUNG SAM: A gardener

NARRATOR 2: A gentleman who is a gardener.

(An OLDER WOMAN *who has been seated with a young gigolo rises and slaps her companion.)*

OLDER WOMAN. Why do I do this to myself? *(To* LILA *and* YOUNG SAM.*)* Love is for fools.

NARRATOR: Love is for…

OLDER WOMAN. On the other hand…

(The OLDER WOMAN *spots the* PLAINCLOTHES MAN. *He beckons. They exit together. The gigolo pouts.)*

YOUNG SAM: I need a photo of your brother, so I'll know him.

LILA: No photos. If there were they'd be out of date. He's been missing for ten years.

YOUNG SAM: How do I recognize him?

LILA: By his habits. Smokes Luckies.

NARRATOR: Smokes Luckies.

LILA: Chews Doublemint gum.

NARRATOR: Doublemint gum.

LILA: He has very light eyes.

NARRATOR: Light eyes.

LILA: He needs his medicine.

NARRATOR: Needs his medicine.

CLUB SINGER: Needs his medicine.

LILA: Got it?

YOUNG SAM: Got it.

LILA: Find him, Sam. My brother robbed me of the family inheritance. I could have opened a beauty salon in Market Square, instead of working in this dump.

YOUNG SAM: When I find him, how do I get the money?

LILA: Ask him for it.

YOUNG SAM: What if he won't give it to me?

LILA: Take it.

YOUNG SAM: Right. Take it.

LILA. Right.

YOUNG SAM: Lila, I love you.

LILA: I know.

YOUNG SAM: When I come back, we'll . .

LILA: Two more people. And the most important. My brother's wife, Darlene. When he disappeared, she went with him. Darlene was a dancer at the Go-Go-Rama Lounge here in Pittsburgh.

(DARLENE *appears. Loud Go-Go music for 10 seconds, as she dances. It cuts off suddenly. She freezes.*)

LILA: She was also a sensitive and intelligent person. She read the poetry of Emily Dickinson between sets.

DARLENE: "I'm nobody. Who are you?"

LILA: Twenty minutes on, twenty minutes off. My brother owned the place. Darlene thought he was a, quote,

DARLENE: Nice guy.

LILA: Unquote. One night Darlene arrived for work to find that the Go-Go-Rama had burnt to the ground.

LILA'S BROTHER. *(On mike, unseen)* Must have been a dissatisfied customer.

LILA: Said my brother. Darlene was not amused. She was out of a job, and the sunglasses she'd left in her dressing room had melted in the blaze.

DARLENE: "Hope is the thing with feathers."

LILA: Said Darlene.

BROTHER: *(On mike, unseen)* Yeah.

LILA: Said my brother.

BROTHER: *(On mike, unseen)* But I owe people.

DARLENE: We'll think of something.

LILA: Said Darlene.

BROTHER: *(On mike, unseen)* Yeah.

LILA: Said my brother, and called a cab to take her home. At six-thirty A M, as Darlene was dreaming of an Aztec City, the phone rang. My brother had been arrested for setting fire to his own club for the insurance money.

BROTHER: *(On mike, unseen)* They're holding me on Easter Island.

NARRATOR: Said my brother.

BROTHER: *(On mike, unseen)* Visiting hours are two to four.

LILA: Darlene thought she'd cheer him up. He was expecting her. There was a circle in the glass…

(As LILA *says the following,* DARLENE *alone mimes this prison visitor room conversation.)*

LILA: His mouth, her ear. Her mouth, his ear. His mouth, her ear. Her mouth, his ear…Darlene married my brother. Then they disappeared.

*(*DARLENE *is gone. Handing* JAKE's *gun to* YOUNG SAM.*)*

LILA: Take this. You might need it.

YOUNG SAM: What? I don't even know how to…

LILA: Watch out for the Bottler!

YOUNG SAM: Who?

ALL: THE BOTTLER!

YOUNG SAM: Who's the Bottler?

LILA: Remember. Get your man, get his money, and get out. When you come back, I'll be waiting for you…

3

YOUNG SAM: To prepare myself for finding Lila's missing brother, I wrote for an instruction cassette from the Universal Detective Agency and College. Lesson One.

(A group of actors—the "lesson cassette," surrounds YOUNG SAM. Various voices and effects are "on the cassette:" i.e., sounds of footsteps, machine guns, and the lesson itself. The lesson is performed by various voices, on mike.)

CASSETTE: THE MISSING PERSON KNOWS WHERE HE HIMSELF IS. THE ONLY TROUBLE IS THAT YOUR CLIENT DOES NOT KNOW.

YOUNG SAM: Playback.

CASSETTE: *(Different voice)* …DOES NOT KNOW. The missing person often seems as if he has had a chunk of his mind removed, like a slice out of a watermelon.

(A slice of watermelon appears. Women's voices, alternating;)

CASSETTE: I D POINTS: scars, tattoos, hair, moustache.

YOUNG SAM: Stop. Start.

CASSETTE: Beard, limp, dragging walk. Brand of gum. Brand of smokes. Et cetera.

YOUNG SAM: Playback.

CASSETTE: Et cetera. D O R—Discharged on own recognizance, D O B—Date of birth. *(Man's voice:)* D O A—Dead on arrival.

YOUNG SAM: Playback.

CASSETTE: Dead on arrival. *(Woman's voice:)* Don't drink on the job. Unless you've been specifically invited to join your client for meals, bring your own sandwiches and coffee. Keep your coat and tie on, unless someone invites you to remove them. Allow no one to examine your gun. Don't take it out of its holster unless you intend to shoot someone. Don't shoot someone unless you intend to kill him. *(All)* No one vanishes without a trace. *(Man's voice:)* This trace may be small, hard to find, but it's there. The only people you may never be able to find are the very criminal, the very rich, or the very dead.

YOUNG SAM: Stop.

CASSETTE: *(Women.)* That's all.

(The "cassette" is gone. OLD SAM *appears in another area, his hotel room.)*

OLD SAM: That stuff about her brother was the most interesting thing Lila ever said to me. Something deep in me was interested. He sounds like a guy who might be worth my time…

YOUNG SAM: He's missing from the world—so he must be nutso, or he's got amnesia, or he's scared. So I figure he won't be too much trouble over Lila's dough. The trouble is finding him. But I can work on the way… ain't my usual route, but what the hell. So, I pack a nice selection of novelties outta the Apex catalog…so it shouldn't be a total loss…

(YOUNG SAM *packs novelties as* OLD SAM *speaks. We see goozelum goggles [the kind of glasses where the eyeballs dangle on springs], x-ray specs, joy buzzer, etc.)*

OLD SAM: So it shouldn't be a total loss…I sell those things to amuse. People need something. I mean, if you work for a living, you are probably not thanking God every morning for giving you the gift of life. I mean the kids are spilling the Wheaties all over the table, and the old lady don't look so good…I mean we don't live in magazines. I live here. Alone. I get up in the morning and drink God's coffee and here I am. Sherman Arms…and there you are with everything you got, and everything you don't got hanging around your neck, and then a Chinese fingertrap comes into your life… vampire teeth…a joy buzzer. Stupid little things. They work—cause of people's ideas. These gags break the rules in people's heads. If there weren't any rules, I'd be outta business.

(YOUNG SAM *finishes packing, closes his case.)*

YOUNG SAM: I guess I'm going. I must love her like crazy.

NARRATOR: At the travel agency, Scene 12.

(The TRAVEL AGENT *and his female* ASSISTANT. *She is holding a map of the world.)*

AGENT: Port Desire, you say?

YOUNG SAM: Yeah.

AGENT: *(Looking on world map.)* We can't send you there if we can't find the place. Be sensible. How about Australia?

ASSISTANT: HA HA HA.

YOUNG SAM: Look again, will ya. That's the world. It's gotta be there somewhere.

AGENT: Ah! There's the little bugger. Port Desire. Sorry. You can't get there from here.

ASSISTANT: HA HA HA.

AGENT: However, I can send you to Port Satisfaction, which is right in the Port Desire neighborhood, sailing today on the *S S Guernsey.*

ALL: Mooo! Moo!

YOUNG SAM: Sounds like a cattle boat.

AGENT: Certainly. Extra fare.

YOUNG SAM: Extra fare?

AGENT: Worth it, believe me. You travel with prize-winning cattle, and they put a bed in your stall.

ASSISTANT: HA HA HA.

YOUNG SAM: All right, dammit. How do I find the boat?

AGENT: Go down to Pier 52, and follow the flies.

ASSISTANT: HA HA HA.

AGENT: By the way, *(Takes our large hypodermic.)* do you have your inoculations? Ten bucks. You're travelling with pureblood cattle and the owners don't wanna take no chances...

(YOUNG SAM leaves the agency, avoiding the AGENT, who pursues him with his hypo. The AGENT is gone. Music, as YOUNG SAM moves down a line of dancing farewell well-wishers, with Lila at the end of the line. They give advice as they dance past him.)

MUSIC: *(Song)*
The wheel of fortune, keeps spinning around,
Will the arrow point my way, etc.

MAN: People want blood for ten cents.

DARLENE: I'm nobody. Who are you?

LAUNDRYMAN: No tickee, no washee.

(LILA *kisses him.*)

LILA: Sam—be careful.

YOUNG SAM: Lila...I . . .

LILA: Get your man, get his money, and get out

(*Music, "The Wheel of Fortune", continuing. All wave.*
YOUNG SAM *exits.*)

4

(*The lighthouse keeper and his dog, inside their lighthouse,
the dog to be played by an actress. The light above them
sweeps 360°.*)

NARRATOR: At the lighthouse, scene 27.

KEEPER: This is the Port Desire Lighthouse. I'm all
alone here.

DOG: Bow wow.

KEEPER: With my faithful dog. We haven't seen a soul
for five months and thirty days. Only a boat or two in
the distance...cruise liners.

(*A boat appears.*)

KEEPER: I can spot them through this telescope, playing
shuffleboard on deck... Red in ten! Six month shift.
Captain said he'd bring out something to cheer me up
when he came to relieve me. Don't need it. My nerves
are steady. (*Holds out hand.*) That'll show Captain.
"Ignore the visions," he told me. I told him he had
nothing to worry about. I've never felt better in my life.

(*The boat is gone.*)

KEEPER: I've learned to love it here... Out here we
breathe the sea mist.

(KEEPER *takes deep breaths, as does the* "DOG".)

KEEPER: The sea mist is half air, half saltwater. It rises up off the waves. It's been breathed by pelicans, by tuna, by krakens. It purifies us of all evil thoughts, puts us in touch with something deeper, stronger. And we're safe here. Safe. These cylindrical walls are thirty feet thick. No storm ever born could shake these walls. Safer than in church.

DOG: Bow wow.

(Storm begins. Thunder, rain)

KEEPER: Uh oh. Wind is up. *(Peers through telescope)* Must be thirty miles an hour. Black clouds on the horizon. The waves look higher than I've ever seen them before.

(A voice from below…)

YOUNG SAM: *(Shouting through storm)* Hello! Hello!

KEEPER: What?

YOUNG SAM: Hello! There's a storm out here! Let me in! My life is in danger out here.

KEEPER: Who are you?

YOUNG SAM: My Uncle Sam. I got some things here you might like! Novelties! Knick knacks! Funmakers! Open the damn door!

(KEEPER *lets* YOUNG SAM *in.*)

DOG: Bow wow.

YOUNG SAM: Yeah… Uh, thank you. You the lighthouse keeper?

KEEPER: Now about those things…

YOUNG SAM: I got party favors? Tricks? Puzzles? Household helpers? No, hah. You say you want more for your money? You say that what you've heard so far just ain't enough. Tell you what I'm gonna do.

This— *(He shows it.)* —is the luminous crucifix. A recent advance in chemical technology has transformed the home crucifix from a piece of bric-a-brac to this living symbol of Christ's agony. The time for prayer is the nighttime, when the cares of the day are ended. The difficulty has been that it's impossible, at night, to see the ordinary crucifix. In the darkest room, this cross of perpetual light gives a wonderful warming glow, representing the luminous body of Jesus. What a comfort to the children on a stormy night. And this luminosity is not only lasting. It is permanent.

DOG: Bow wow.

YOUNG SAM: Next time you see me, you're gonna thank me. How many can I put you down for?

KEEPER: One.

YOUNG SAM: Just the one?

KEEPER: *(With a look at his dog.)* Two.

(Thunder. The storm builds.)

YOUNG SAM: By the way, I'm looking for a friend of mine…he used to work here, I think. Lila's brother.

KEEPER: Lila's brother? I remember him. Someone named Jake was here asking questions about him. He said he'd hurt me if I didn't tell. He didn't have to do that, did he?

YOUNG SAM: Did you tell him?

KEEPER: Breathe! Breathe the sea mist! Ah…that's better. You know, Lila's brother was the best man who ever ran the light.

YOUNG SAM: Where did he go from here?

KEEPER: He wasn't afraid of the tower, the rocks, the evil music of the gulls.

YOUNG SAM: Where is he now?

KEEPER: Got any gum?

YOUNG SAM: Gum?

KEEPER: Doublemint. It's my favorite.

NARRATOR: The missing man has a chunk of his mind removed, like a slice out of a watermelon.

(The watermelon appears.)

KEEPER: Got any gum?

YOUNG SAM: Gum?

KEEPER: Doublemint. It's my favorite.

YOUNG SAM: I've only got exploding gum. By the way, do you have a sister?

KEEPER: I'm an only child. Can't you tell?

(The watermelon is gone.)

YOUNG SAM: Then just tell me, where did Lila's brother go?

KEEPER: I like you. You should stay here. I'll teach you everything...how to work the light, how to breathe in the salty mist. You'll be safe, like we are. I'll teach you the language of the gulls, caught between heaven and earth.

DOG: Bow wow.

(In the distance, a boat appears.)

PASSENGERS: FUN! FUN! FUN! FUN! . . .

YOUNG SAM: *(Aside.)* This guy's a jerk.

BOAT CAPTAIN: Meanwhile, on the approaching boat, bringing the lighthouse relief crew, a fabulous party is in progress.

PASSENGERS: FUN! FUN! FUN! FUN! FUN! FUN! FUN! FUN!

(The PASSENGERS, *including the* BOAT CAPTAIN, *pile into the lighthouse, begin to crawl lasciviously around and over the dog, lighthouse keeper, and* YOUNG SAM. YOUNG SAM *backs away. Thunder.)*

KEEPER: The sea mist! The walls!

YOUNG SAM: *(Shouting)* Where did he go? Lila's brother?

ALL: FUN! FUN! FUN!

KEEPER: To the University! Professor Finley!

YOUNG SAM: The University. Professor Finley. Thanks a lot.

Sea mist, my ass.

DOG: Bow wow.

*(*YOUNG SAM *backs away from the orgy in progress as all lights fade but the lighthouse light, cries of passion mix with thunder as the storm builds. A last glimpse of the lighthouse, as it begins to topple, party and all, into the sea.)*

5

(A LITTLE PERSON *by the side of the road, wearing a dirty yellow vest. Nearby, a device for showing magic lantern slides, essentially a box with a peephole, with a place to insert a large glass slide. From below the box hangs a sign: See the World. 10 cents.)*

LITTLE PERSON: *(Singing)* The wheel of fortune, keeps spinning around… *(Holds up, points to a slide.)* Peasants on the Yangtzee.

(The LITTLE PERSON *inserts it, sits.* JAKE *enters.)*

JAKE: This the road to the university?

LITTLE PERSON: May be. See the world?

JAKE: I'm seeing enough of it already.

LITTLE PERSON: Got a butt? Got any food? Got any money?

JAKE: Get out of my way, pops.

LITTLE PERSON: Why you going to college? Ain't you educated yet?

JAKE: None of your business. *(He shoves the* LITTLE PERSON *aside, exits.)*

NARRATOR: A GARDEN INTERLUDE! With Mister Capability Brown.

*(*CAPABILITY BROWN *enters. 18th century costume)*

CAPABILITY BROWN: I perceive that these grounds have never been touched by the finger of taste. Allow me to wave over them the wand of enchantment. These rocks shall be blown up, these trees cut down, and the wilderness with all its goats and monkeys will vanish like mist. A garden shall rise upon its ruins.

NARRATOR: Mister Capability Brown was a master of space.

CAPABILITY BROWN: I am a master of space.

NARRATOR: What's missing for most gardeners to make them feel like artists, is a sufficiently harebrained plan.

CAPABILITY BROWN: A true garden provides settings for sensation, reflection, and repose. It must contain summer hermitages, winter hermitages, terminaries, bowling greens, Chinese pavilions, natural grottos, cascades, mosques, huts, pagodas, rustic seats and Druidical temples, many of which may be executed with flints, irregular stones, rude branches, or the roots of trees. An Eden to live in. I intend to create this Elysium in this very countryside, and to…

NARRATOR. END OF GARDEN INTERLUDE.

(CAPABILITY BROWN *is gone. The* LITTLE PERSON *is still on stage. In the distance,* OLD SAM *appears. He is looking into a Viewmaster.* YOUNG SAM *enters.*)

LITTLE PERSON: *(Singing to self)* The wheel of fortune, is spinning around...

YOUNG SAM: Excuse me, is this the way to the university?

LITTLE PERSON: Maybe. See the world?

YOUNG SAM: Thanks, but I'm doing O K on my own.

LITTLE PERSON: Think so? You got a butt?

YOUNG SAM: Yeah...but it's my last one.

LITTLE PERSON: Can I have it?

YOUNG SAM: *(Hesitating)* Sure. Here. Have a nice day. *(Handing a cigarette)*

LITTLE PERSON: What happened to your face?

YOUNG SAM: Wha...Nothing. I mean . . .

LIME PERSON. Watch out for room 33.

YOUNG SAM: What?

LITTLE PERSON: You're a nice boy. Going to school?

YOUNG SAM: To the university.

LITTLE PERSON: When you're there, go dancing.

YOUNG SAM: Dancing?

LITTLE PERSON: Keep moving, give all of yourself away. You're a nice boy. These days, people want blood for ten cents. Get it, too.

YOUNG SAM: Do they? What else you got to say?

LITTLE PERSON: Be careful. Watch our for the Bottler.

YOUNG SAM: Who?

LITTLE PERSON: THE BOTTLER.

YOUNG SAM: *(Aside.)* I've heard that before. *(To* LITTLE PERSON.*)* Any other words of wisdom?

LITTLE PERSON: Yeah. Don't let your mouth write no check that your tail can't cash. *(The Little Person returns the cigarette Young Sam gave. He takes it.)*

YOUNG SAM: Thanks, I guess.

(Blackout.)

6

(The BOTTLER, MISS SIMMONS *[dressed in violet],* MR FLEAGLE, *and the body of* JAKE.*)*

NARRATOR 1: There were four people in a room at the Ramada Inn. Room 33. One of them had been shot several times in the chest. The people who shot him were not exactly green peas at their business. He lay across an orange bedspread and blood bubbled in his throat. He was about to die.

FLEAGLE: Fucker's taking his time about it.

NARRATOR 1: The dying man, except for the blood that soaked his shirt front, was just another tough guy with a bald spot—although he had more stamina than most tough guys with bald spots. He was dying hard.

JAKE: Uggghhhhh. Uggghhhh.

MISS SIMMONS: He's going. Maybe, Fleagle, you went too far.

BOTTLER: Ask him again.

*(*MISS SIMMONS *slaps* JAKE *hard across the face.)*

MISS SIMMONS: *(To* JAKE*)* Talk to me, darling. I love you. Any man in pain is so attractive…It's hopeless.

NARRATOR 2: *(The* AUTHOR*)* The group in this room would stand out in a crowd of ordinary humans like whores in church. Miss Simmons had gone out to the far east in her youth, as a governess, but once in Hong Kong, she soon found other occupations. She was even a singer once, at a place outside of Pittsburgh called the Neptune Inn.

MISS SIMMONS: *(Singing)* Whose honey are youuuuu

NARRATOR 3: A lady in a violet gown...

NARRATOR 2: *(The* AUTHOR*)* Mister Fleagle had been a clerk in a banking firm in Allentown, Pennsylvania. His very ingenious system of embezzlement obtained his discharge. The bank president was found some days later, the victim of a hideous freak accident involving a toaster and a high voltage line.

*(*FLEAGLE *hisses at the* NARRATOR.*)*

NARRATOR 2: *(The* AUTHOR*)* This is the Bottler. No one knows anything for certain about the Bottler. Perhaps he used to be a business partner of Lila's father. The Bottler does seem to feel that something belonging to him has gone astray, and that Lila's brother has it, and could be persuaded to return it—if he could only find him *(Exits)*

FLEAGLE: Finish him. He won't remember anything else.

MISS SIMMONS: Yeah. Let's get out of here. This room gives me the creeps.

FLEAGLE: Let's get on the other guy she sent out. I'm itching for it. I want that do-re-mi in my pocket as I percolate down the boulevard, with my entire residue behind me.

MISS SIMMONS: Fleagle, you are nowhere, you will be nowhere, and you can't be anywhere, as you are nowhere in front.

FLEAGLE: Shut up, you stupid bitch.

BOTTLER: Quiet. *(Looking at* JAKE*)* Jake, memory is like an old music box. It lies silent for years, and then a mere nothing, a tremor will start the dusty spring, and the melody plays once more. Remember, Jake. What else did she tell you? Some memories are stirred by the sight of a faded flower, a hotel bill—a sudden stab of pain...the sound of a voice, a bar of music, a flavor on the tongue... It seems he's dead.

FLEAGLE: I didn't know the gun was loaded.

BOTTLER., He had nothing more to tell us. Just another one of Lila's fiancés...though this one got further than most..."The University" ...That's all he remembered from the bitch's instructions... Hmmmmm.

MISS SIMMONS: I'm nervous. Let's get out of here.

(Lights out, and up on YOUNG SAM *approaching a hotel desk.)*

YOUNG SAM: I'm beat. Better check in and get some sleep.

CLERK: Yes.

YOUNG SAM: I'd like a . .

CLERK: *(Handing key)* Room 33. Pleasant dreams.

*(*CLERK *is gone.* YOUNG SAM *enters room 33. It's empty.)*

YOUNG SAM: Room 33. Uh oh. Looks normal enough. *(Takes out* JAKE'*s gun.)* Better be on the safe side. Hey, maybe the man I'm looking for lay here...Lila's brother—the missing man. Was he awake all night... frightened? Or sleeping? Dreaming? Is he dreaming me following him? I'm a spectre in his sleep... Is he angry? Is he laughing? Or crying? Has he lost his way?

*(*JAKE'*s body falls out of the closet with a crash...)*

YOUNG SAM: I've seen him somewhere before.

(The phone rings.)

YOUNG SAM: Hello, My Uncle Sam here, novelties, notions…Lila!

(Lights up on LILA *in another area, with phone.)*

YOUNG SAM: It's you! …O K… Right… Right… Uh, this guy Jake is here. Yeah, I've seen him in the club. He's dead. What do you think he's doing here?…Me neither….O K. Lila—I love you.

(LILA *hangs up phone. Lights dim on* YOUNG SAM *in room.)*

LILA: I know. Cry and you'll get a red nose, Lila my darling. Jake's dead. And Sam… *(At a mirror, dressing up to go out)* Not bad, Lila my darling. Only one left now, and he needs all the help he can find. Just get yourself together, go out into the world and make yourself as welcome as a snowflake in hell.

TRAVEL AGENT. *(With map of world)* Where to, Miss?

(Blackout. Lights up on…)

7

COLLEGE CHEERLEADERS: *(Cheer)* Be aggressive, Be Aggressive B-E-A-G-G! R-E-S-S-I-V-E!

NARRATOR: AT THE UNIVERSITY, scene 14.

YOUNG SAM: Before I get there .

ANOTHER NARRATOR. Stella! *(As* STELLA *enters.)* Her furnished room wasn't very far from the university. Now she stands gazing out over the college town, smiling a triumphant smile.

STELLA: Fundamentals of Botany. That's one course I won't have to worry about anymore.

NARRATOR: Stella opens the closet, unhooks a slinky black cocktail dress from the rack…

STELLA: It's time to roll out the big guns.

MITZI: *(Coming in.)* Stella! Say, where are you going?

NARRATOR: It was Mitzi, Stella's roommate.

STELLA: Got a heavy date tonight, Mitzi.

MITZI: It isn't a blind date, I hope. I wouldn't fool around with any blind dates these days.

STELLA: Oh cut it out, Mitzi. So three girls disappear from campus. Is that any reason to start ugly rumors about murderers and maniacs?

MITZI: I didn't start the rumors, Stella. Who's the guy?

STELLA: Professor Finley.

MITZI: Finley? The botany teacher? Are you out of your mind? He's an old creep.

STELLA: He may be an old creep, Mitz, but if I don't pass Botany, I don't graduate, and what I know about botany wouldn't fill a thimble.

MITZI: I get it...

STELLA: Not a word. I promised him I wouldn't tell a soul.

MITZI: Don't worry, honey, your secret romance is safe with me. *(She exits.)*

STELLA: Poor Professor Finley. If he only knew what he's letting himself in for...

(Professor FINLEY enters, moving slowly toward STELLA. He caresses a plant.)

NARRATOR: Stella had planned it all carefully, ever since that first week when they'd covered roots and stems, and she knew, with pistils and stamens still to come, she'd never be able to pass. She'd worn her sexiest outfits to class, sat in the front row, and finally he'd bitten...

STELLA: You wanted to see me, Professor?

FINLEY: I read your paper on chlorophyll, Miss Sharp. Frankly, I'm worried about how much you've grasped from my lectures.

STELLA: I'm a little worried myself, Professor. Perhaps if you reviewed it for me, say some evening...

FINLEY: That would be highly irregular, Miss Sharp. The faculty frowns on fraternization.

STELLA: Well, I wouldn't want to get you into any trouble.

FINLEY: Perhaps if no one knew...if it was our little secret. I mean I'd like to help you, Miss Sharp. You're a very nice...girl.

NARRATOR: He'd taken the bait. Hook, line, and sinker.

FINLEY: Shall we say, tonight. At eight. At my house.

STELLA: Oh Professor! This is so sweet of you. I could kiss you...

(FINLEY *exits.*)

NARRATOR: Professor Finley's house was one of those old piles that had been fashionable a century ago. Stella walks through the dark garden, up the steps, lifts the huge door knocker, and the hollow sound echoes down long corridors, dies away in dark corners within. The door creaks open.

FINLEY: Why, Miss Sharp. You're all dressed up.

STELLA: Just a little something I picked up for cocktails. Like it?

FINLEY: It's a very nice gown, Miss Sharp. Come in.

STELLA: Call me Stella, Professor.

FINLEY: Would you care for a drink—Stella?

STELLA: Why, thanks.

NARRATOR: The wine was sweet, syrupy, with a heavy aroma. The corridor was dark, as Stella followed Professor Finley down...down...toward a wooden door covered with odd carvings. The nagging thought that she was alone with this strange old man...Those three girls who disappeared so recently? ...Had they been students in Finley's Botany class? She couldn't remember.... That wine he'd given her must have gone to her head. Finley opened the door, and as they stepped inside, Stella could hear the click of the lock behind her. At one end of the room, the floor was covered with earth. Growing in the earth—twisted green things with bulbous crimson tops pulsating open and shut like lecherous mouths...

STELLA: Ooooooooh!

FINLEY: Yes, Stella! Flesh eating plants are my forte. These are native to the Amazon. These plants Stella, they need life! They need blood and flesh, Stella...*(As he picks her up to throw her into plants.)* Their digestion is a fascinating process, I assure you...

STELLA: Oh NO!!! AHHHHHHH!

YOUNG SAM: *(Entering.)* Excuse me? Professor Finley?
FINLEY. Yes?

YOUNG SAM: I'm My Uncle Sam.

FINLEY: This is Stella. *(Putting her down to shake Sam's hand)* May I ask what you're doing here?

YOUNG SAM: Uh...I've got a few novelty items here— *(Opening suitcase)* I thought you and the little lady might find interesting to have around the home. Start your own Ant Farm. Watch them work, worship and play! Goozelum Goggles!

FINLEY: Do you think a university professor would be interested in Goozelum Goggles?

(Behind FINLEY's back, STELLA exits.)

YOUNG SAM: You're a big reader, I bet.

FINLEY: Of course I am.

YOUNG SAM: Tell you what I'm gonna do. Special
price for you and the missus on any of the selection
of exciting books I have to offer. Here's one called
Confessions of a Nun...this one's written in the kind
of plain language anyone can understand. I can see
you're a man of the world. Here's a copy of "From
Ballroom to Hell" by an ex-dance teacher...awful
dangers to young girls in the dancing academy. How
about HIRAM BIRDSEED AT THE WORLD'S FAIR?
(Aside to audience.) This Hiram Birdseed at the World's
Fair is my biggest seller. These books are all published
by the same company in Philadelphia. For men only.
You know the kind—*Sam Savage in the South Seas*..."the
naked maidens surrounded him..." and so on. It's like
the same guy wrote them all, though they got different
names on 'em. But Hiram Birdseed is different. It's like
this writer of all of them was hit by fantasy exhaustion
one day and he hadda stay in bed, so for one time
they hired another guy...a little guy with a dirty green
cardigan sweater and glasses, and he was given this
title, Hiram Birdseed at the World's Fair, and the idea:
farm boy gets involved in international sex in New
York City, and this little guy goes back to his furnished
room, and he writes. He stays up all night, his mind
at white heat, and as the dawn filters through the
venetian blinds he finishes the first half. He falls into
a fitful doze. The pages on the desk flutter in an early
morning breeze...In the first half of this book, Hiram
Birdseed does not even get to the world's fair. He does
not even get to New York. In chapter one, he's on the
farm. He looks at a cow sleeping. In the second chapter
he eats breakfast. A page and a half details how the
gravy looks dripping over the biscuits. The third
chapter is called Hiram Birdseed's Dream. There's a

glowing garden of unearthly trees in which Chinamen in violet robes are tormenting this porcupine with long golden sticks. By the time you get to about page ninety eight, Hiram is at last on a train to New York, and he's looking at the blonde hairs on the back of the neck of a girl seated in front of him. Then suddenly the style changes, like the old hack rose up our of his sickbed in horror, and took over. All at once, Little Egypt is shakin' it, and Hiram, the same Hiram who watched the cow sleep in chapter one, is watching the bouncing breasts. *(To* FINLEY*)* My best seller.

FINLEY: You're a bright boy, but you don't actually know anything—do you? Why don't you enroll. Here at the university there's knowledge, sex, and the companionship of intelligent minds.

YOUNG SAM: I'll think it over. Got a cigarette?

FINLEY: Of course. Luckies are my brand. You don't mind?

NARRATOR: Smokes Luckies.

YOUNG SAM: Not at all. By the way, does the name Lila mean anything to you?

FINLEY: No.

YOUNG SAM: How about "Lila's brother"?

FINLEY: Brilliant boy. An ex-student of mine. "A" in my graduate botany seminar. Quite the inventive geneticist. Then he dropped out. Pity.

YOUNG SAM: Yeah. What a shame. Look, I'm trying to find him, and I need to know where…

FINLEY: *(Looks at watch)* You'll have to excuse me. It's time for my dance class.

DANCE TEACHER: Ready! Everybody in place!

(All company, but YOUNG SAM, *prepare to dance. The* BOTTLER, MISS SIMMONS *and* FLEAGLE *together on an end*

of the dance class away from YOUNG SAM *and* FINLEY. OLD SAM *and* LILA *on opposite sides, toward the rear.)*

YOUNG SAM: I'm not here for the class. I just...
TEACHER. IN PLACE! CHIN UP! SHOULDERS
BACK! GUT IN! Thank you—

*(*YOUNG SAM *gets in line with the whole class, next to* FINLEY. *Music: Cha cha cha.)*

DANCE TEACHER: ONE TWO CHA CHA CHA, THREE FOUR CHA CHA CHA, TURN AND CHA CHA CHA.

MAN IN CLASS: A gentleman with eight flags.

YOUNG SAM: *(Still dancing)* What?

ANOTHER MAN IN CLASS: A gentleman with a big book.

YOUNG SAM: *(To* FINLEY*)* What? Professor, where did he go?

FINLEY: Who?

YOUNG SAM: Lila's brother!

FINLEY: Try Chinatown.

YOUNG SAM: Chinatown?

FINLEY: Yes. Needs his medicine— Follow my laundry man.

DANCE TEACHER: ONE TWO CHA CHA CHA...

(The Chinese LAUNDRYMAN *appears, a large bag of laundry on his shoulder. He exits.* YOUNG SAM *separates himself from the dancers, exits, following the laundryman. He in turn is followed off by the* BOTTLER's *trio. All other dancers leave except* LILA *and* OLD SAM. *He watches her. She exits.* OLD SAM *alone, cha-chas hesitantly, then more strongly as the music builds. Blackout. Lights up as* YOUNG SAM *follows the* LAUNDRYMAN. *He punches a button on his cassette player.)*

CASSETTE: Universal Detective Agency. Missing Persons, lesson 2...

*(During the following "Play" of the cassette, performed
by the company on mike, as* YOUNG SAM *follows the*
LAUNDRYMAN *to Chinatown, the* BOTTLER, MISS
SIMMONS, *and* FLEAGLE *appear and follow him.)*

CASSETTE: To locate the missing man, it is often
necessary to employ the basic techniques of
shadowing, or, tailing. There are two kinds of tail: the
close tail, where your main concern is not to lose the
subject, and the loose tail where your main concern
is not to be spotted. If your subject spots you, you've
blown it. Avoid this. Look ordinary. Leave those flashy
clothes at home. Disguises should be simple: a hat, or
a pair of glasses. A subject who is suspicious may use
windows or mirrors to try to spot you. The investigator
may even find himself followed by someone trying to
find out why he's following someone else. Avoid this.
If you think you're being followed, go into a theatre or
restaurant and out another door. Above all—identify
with the missing man.

(All followers freeze.)

CASSETTE: What would you do if you were him? Where
would you go? It's easy. After all, we're all missing.
The only difference is for how long…a minute of
daydreaming in an unfamiliar park or garden .. a half
hour in a strange bar and grill when no one knows
where you are. You're gone. Before you know it, you're
on a bus…a new city…a new name. Missing. Don't get
confused by the meaning of it all. Do your job.

(All followers again begin to follow each other.)

CASSETTE: Do what you were sent for. That's all.

(The LAUNDRYMAN *exits.* YOUNG SAM *follows. The*
BOTTLER, MISS SIMMONS *and* FLEAGLE *follow him.)*

8

(An opium den, its DENIZENS *scattered about on low bunks, smoking set-ups next to them. One of them stares into a Viewmaster. They smoke. An elderly Chinese center, the owner, with a parrot on her shoulder.)*

DENIZEN 1: Do not think ill of me for frequenting this place. Remember times when you too wanted to disappear, to find a place where the world could never reach you. That place is only in your mind, when the smoky walls swing shut and you live within....I have been a visitor here for years. After all, my dreams are harmless enough...

NARRATOR: A bad poet.

DENIZEN 1: This room is place of passage between the worlds...

DENIZEN 2: *(A woman singing)* The wheel of fortune, keeps spinning 'round...

DENIZEN 3: ...she was eaten by raccoons, or beavers or something...

(The LAUNDRYMAN *enters, takes a pipe from the* OWNER, *lies down.)*

NARRATOR: The owner of the place is a cultivated chink. An opium peddler, yes, but also a philosopher.

OWNER: Ugliness and beauty are opposites. But when the black smoke fills your head, one is as good as the other.

*(*YOUNG SAM *enters.)*

YOUNG SAM: This is an opium den!

DENIZEN 4: As Brother Brigham said when he crossed the border into Utah... Children, this is the place!

YOUNG SAM: Maybe some of the gang would be interested in purchasing a few entertaining...

DENIZEN 4: They're only interested in their medicine.

YOUNG SAM: O K, O K. Then I'll get right to the point. I'm looking for Lila's brother...

DENIZEN 4: Quiet. Quiet, before someone slits your throat. He was here. He's gone, long ago. He ascended from this house devoted to ruin—up to the third heaven...

YOUNG SAM: Where?

DENIZEN 3: Shh... Everyone here has already heard your stupid braying...in their dreams. Have a pipe... and wait.

OWNER: You seek the black smoke?...

(OWNER *hands* YOUNG SAM *the pipe. He lies on a bunk, waits.* MISS SIMMONS *enters. Approaches* YOUNG SAM.)

NARRATOR: (OLD SAM *from a bunk.*) Then she appeared. She flowed across the room like hot molasses. She sat down, crossed her legs slow, gentle, taking care not to bruise any of that smooth tender flesh. She had lips that would burn holes in asbestos. She smiled, but she didn't say anything. Maybe she couldn't talk. Maybe she was an idiot. I didn't care.

YOUNG SAM: (*To* MISS SIMMONS) Lady, whatever it is, it's eight to five I'll do it.

MISS SIMMONS: You're right, but I'd say even money.

YOUNG SAM: I'm My Uncle Sam... You come here often?

OLD SAM: Miss Simmons was able to project a fatal combination...a capacity for unending self absorbed sensual pleasure, and a cute little fear of this capacity in herself that could let a man be a man. Deadly. For a moment, she drove Lila completely out of my head.

MISS SIMMONS: Shhh. Let's smoke a pipe. I love to suck the black smoke into my brain.

YOUNG SAM: I never tried this stuff...though I always suspected that the chinks in Yip Man's Chinese Laundry in Pittsburgh were using the stuff in the back room...

LAUNDRYMAN: *(In another area)* Hey, Wong! Take the iron for awhile, and let me have the pipe...

OLD SAM: Other devotees of the black smoke optically fondled Miss Simmons as we puffed away. They mumbled in their stupor.

DENIZEN: ...gentleman with eight flags...

OTHER DENIZEN: ...gentleman with a big book...

OLD SAM: My head was getting heavy...

(YOUNG SAM *slips down onto* MISS SIMMONS' *lap. She slips his gun out of his pocket, signals.* BOTTLER *and* FLEAGLE *enter.*)

ALL: THE BOTTLER!

BOTTLER: Thank you.

(BOTTLER *looks down at* YOUNG SAM *in his opium dream.* MISS SIMMONS *hands him* YOUNG SAM's *gun.*)

BOTTLER: So this is My Uncle Sam. Lila's last chance. He's having a delightful dream. If we wish to interview him, we must wake him up. I doubt all of us will disappear. Fleagle!

(FLEAGLE *slaps* YOUNG SAM *around until he wakes.*)

FLEAGLE: Filthy hophead.

BOTTLER: Why do I do this, you ask me. Why?

YOUNG SAM: Who the hell are you? *(Silence)* Are you Lila's brother? *(Hysterical laughter)*

BOTTLER: Sorry. I'm the Bottler.

YOUNG SAM: The Bottler?

FLEAGLE: He's a bright boy.

MISS SIMMONS: Very.

BOTTLER: To continue. Why do I do this? Faster horses?
Younger women? For love? For wisdom? No. I need
that few million in green Lila's brother's got because—I
have a dream. The Bottler's dream. To put it shit
simple, I intend to create paradise on earth. I was left
a little spit of land in Florida in my father's will. From
this prenatal strip of sand will rise, like Venus out of
the sea, *CHEZ BOTTLER,* the finest resort hotel and
casino operation in the hemisphere. Think of it!

YOUNG SAM: I'm thinking of it.

BOTTLER: Every room will have a heart-shaped bathtub
with jacuzzi, steam, carpeting three inches thick, wall
and ceiling mirrors, a king size bed equipped with
magic fingers, and a projection video unit wired in
direct to my library of erotic classics, including Quick
Henry the Flit, Doctor Kremser, Vivisectionist, and
Pom Pom Girls Go Crazy. Each room will also be
equipped with electronic brain stimulation devices
produced simply out of ladies' hairdryers, by my
own patented process. Chez Bottler will have ten
restaurants, including the Undersea Lounge with
a wall size fishtank with dugongs, manatees, and
electric eels. Siamese service personnel, an eclectic
stable of whores, steaks flown in from Kansas City.
Amusements! High stakes baccarat tables, miniature
golf, water polo, lindy-hopping, a zoo, with a petting
area…black swans fly across a red sky, and the moon,
a thin glorious crescent, rises over Chez Bottler! A
warm wind caresses the very stones. In the penthouse
suite sit I, the Bottler, a magnum of champagne in one
hand, a woman's breast in the other, looking out the
window toward the horizon, where the sea touches
the sky. This is the world the Bottler built, God save
him. He came from nothing, and before he goes back
to nothing, he made everything. So three cheers for the

Bottler, my pom pom girls! Miss Simmons, of course, will be in charge of Chez Bottler's social agenda. Fleagle will discipline the staff.

FLEAGLE: I want to push laundry hampers down this carpeted hallway in a red outfit. I want to vacuum...

MISS SIMMONS: I want to walk in the garden, and torment the porcupines with a long golden stick . .

BOTTLER: Shut up. Now, Uncle, tell us—where is Lila's brother?

YOUNG SAM: I don't know. I've been looking for him myself.

BOTTLER: What instructions did Lila give you? What clues?

(YOUNG SAM *is silent*.)

BOTTLER: Mister Fleagle, hit him.

(FLEAGLE *does so, more than once*.)

BOTTLER: Fleagle, restrain yourself. He needs to talk to me. The man has already dropped his hole card.

YOUNG SAM: Lila didn't tell me anything.

BOTTLER: You're lying. Lila tells all her fiances the clues.

YOUNG SAM: What?

BOTTLER: I know her. Take a look.

(BOTTLER *shows* YOUNG SAM *a photo*.)

YOUNG SAM: It's Lila! And she's naked! Where'd you get this?

BOTTLER: I have nude photos of everyone. Talk!

YOUNG SAM: Never!

BOTTLER: I'll find him. I've got a line on his soul, and that line is like a trail of blood in snow. He's dripping blood on the snow for me to follow. He's stolen my dream! When I find him, I will dig his greedy eyes out, and fill the hollow cells with two dim burning bulbs— then place his body by the graveyard gate, to light the coffins in. Fleagle—kill this fool, and catch up to us.

(The BOTTLER *and* MISS SIMMONS *exit. Silence.* FLEAGLE *puts a gun to* YOUNG SAM's *head.)*

FLEAGLE: We'll play American roulette. Put one bullet in, spin the chamber, hold it to the head, and pull the trigger six times. I'll take five seconds between trigger pulls, so you can contemplate the nature of time.

*(*OLD SAM *rises, steps forward to watch. "Click." The* AUTHOR *appears, steps forward to watch. "Click." "Click." The* LITTLE PERSON *in the yellow vest rises up suddenly from a bunk, and rushes toward* FLEAGLE *from behind, a heavy opium pipe raised overhead to strike. All freeze.)*

DENIZEN 1: It is time for another dream, is it not?

*(*DENIZEN 1 *raises a pipe to his lips. Blackout)*

END OF ACT ONE

(Intermission)

ACT TWO

9

(*Darkness. In the dark, voices*)

YOUNG SAM: Hey, I'm sorry your opium den got wrecked, O K. I didn't bring those people here. Look, they beat me up bad. I think my nose is bro...

CHINESE VOICE: How much money you have, my flend?

YOUNG SAM: Money? What about them? The Bottler. The rest of them?

CHINESE VOICE: They are gone. How much?

YOUNG SAM: Thirty bucks.

CHINESE VOICE: That will cover the parrot. How do you intend to pay for the rest of it?

YOUNG SAM: I'm gettin' out of...

(*Sounds of blows, grunts, a beating going on. Sounds fade... The* AUTHOR *appears. He is holding an old-fashioned egg-candler. This is a tin can painted black and rigged up over a lightbulb. A hole to fit the end of an egg into is cut in the side of the can.*)

AUTHOR: My Uncle Sam taught me how to candle eggs. He had never said more than two or three words to me before that Saturday afternoon. He took my hand, and led me down the street to his brother's, my grandfather's, grocery store. Locked. Closed on

Saturday. My Uncle Sam had a key. We went into the
back room, full of old newspapers, and the smell of
cheese. Cool in there. And stacks of eggs in cartons,
ready to be sorted for the bins. Candling eggs. You
stick an egg in the hole, *(Demonstrating)* turn on the
light, and you can see inside the shell…You look for
cracks, or tiny blood spots on the yolk inside. Those
are grade B. The perfect ones are grade A. So there we
were, My Uncle Sam and me, lighting up eggs in the
dark. Once I got the hang of it, Sam sat there on a pile
of newspapers in his cashmere coat and watched me.
He lit a cigar.

(A cigar lights in the dark on stage.)

AUTHOR: I couldn't see him in the dark, but I felt him
watching me, careful, like I shouldn't make a mistake,
and at the same time I had the feeling he was a million
miles away… Now he's still telling his story to himself,
and I'm still telling it to myself, and we're both still
telling it to you. Someone's telling you a story…

(Lights up on OLD SAM. *He's in his hotel room.)*

OLD SAM: Out my window, there's Market Square
below, and beyond it to the west, there's Shady Hill
and the docks by the river, and then the low outline
of the military barracks at Fort Pitt—National Guard.
On some days I can hear the band in the distance,
playing those same bad marches, all the young boys
march forward and back, forward and back. Out
past the barracks, open fields, and on to Florence,
Slovan, west to Steubenville. Over to the east, there's
that green dome of the observatory at the University
of Pittsburgh, where those professors try to spy out
the secrets in the stars, and on past the interstate,
further east to New Alexandria, Wilkinsburg, and
Turtle Creek. To the north, behind my back, the
Monongahela, traffic on the Ninth Street bridge

crossing over by the stadium, out beyond the Jones and
Laughlin stacks to Avalon, then up Route 57 to New
Castle, through to Lake Erie, and across the border
into Canada, where the reindeer roam. Market Square
below, and to the south, the suburbs, breaking up into
scattered patches of tract homes, blurring away to
green and brown, further south past Uniontown and
Wind Ridge, following the river, where it rushes into
the Ohio, and on into the Mississippi, Mississippi to
New Orleans, spreading out through the delta marshes
into the blue Gulf of Mexico, with its shrimps and
sharks, and sailing on over the Caribees, a gull, lost
between heaven and earth, high over the Southern
continent, over Cape Horn, and in the great distance
it all goes white, cold white, and the great sea birds
fly before me into that whiteness and are swallowed,
white on white... I'm not feeling any better. The pain is
everywhere, especially in my chest. It comes and goes.
I can't sleep. The doctors tell me I can't drink. I don't
like T V. So I talk.

(YOUNG SAM *appears, bleeding, dizzy, exhausted.*)

OLD SAM: They left me, behind some billboard. I could
barely stand there and watch myself bleed. Missing
Man, my ass. What about me? I look in my wallet to
remember who I am. Driver's license.

OLD SAM & YOUNG SAM. "My Uncle Sam."

YOUNG SAM: Sounds right. Hey...there's a photo of
somebody's kid in here. It's my nephew's son. He's
three, and he's got a sailor suit on— The moon's
spinning around in little circles— (*He holds his arm. He's
in pain.*) I'm hurt. I got to find a doctor.

(OLD SAM *comes strolling, looking at the moon. A young
boy appears, looking into a View-master.*)

OLD SAM: Nice moon.

YOUNG SAM: Yeah. Uh, Mister, where can I find a doctor?

OLD SAM: Don't you remember?

YOUNG SAM: Remember? I never been...

OLD SAM: Head that way, little house right over the Mexican border. Say, long as I've got your attention here, I happen to have with me a small packet of itching powder. Only ten cents. Sprinkle a little down the ladies' backs at parties.

YOUNG SAM: I'm not going to any parties. Besides, I'm...

OLD SAM: Breaks the ice. Starts the ball rolling. Mix and mingle.

YOUNG SAM: I'm mingling, all right.

OLD SAM: *(Whipping on goozelum goggles.)* How about a pair of goozelum goggles?

YOUNG SAM: *(Opening his case, shows own goggles.)* Look, I'm in the business. How would you like some rubber pretzels? Rubber doughnuts? Try a few on your unsuspecting guests and watch the fun! How many can I put you down for? Now get out of my way. I'm hurt...I need to cross the border, find that doc... *(YOUNG SAM exits. The young boy with the Viewmaster is gone.)*

OLD SAM: Not feeling well, eh. You don't know the half of it... *(To audience)* Punchboard party games? Kissy-kissy? Funny fortune? Nickel a try! *(He coughs.)* Feels like weeds wrapped around my chest here...I better lie down...my younger mind is stifling...like being in a cage full of monkeys, all chattering at once. *(He pulls out a rubber banana.)* These rubber bananas defy detection. EVEN WHEN YOU KNOW, THEY FOOL YOU.

(OLD SAM *exits. The* MEXICAN DOCTOR *appears, along with some equipment.*)

NARRATOR 1: *The Mexican Doctor.* Scene 57.

NARRATOR 2: Common sense suggests that excellent medical care is unlikely to be found in Mexican border towns. However, one never knows, do one?

(YOUNG SAM *enters.*)

YOUNG SAM: The trouble here is that this is actually my life. I mean there is no difference between who I am and who I think I am and who I can make people think I am. This is just it, you know…bleeding into my boots…Doctor!!

DOCTOR: *(Looking him over)* You're not running from the law are you? *Federales*? I'm strictly legitimate.

YOUNG SAM: No. Just patch up this bleeding…

DOCTOR: You can't be too careful with the law. Especially in Sonora. I had an associate who was arrested for pleasuring a pig. In this very state.

YOUNG SAM: What was the charge?

DOCTOR: Rape, of course. But he claimed he had the pig's consent. Complicated case. Still in the courts, I believe. *(He examines* YOUNG SAM.*)* Nasty, nasty. We can take care of you just fine.

(*Lights fade on the* DOCTOR *and* YOUNG SAM, *as in another area, the* BOTTLER's *trio enters, followed by a* NARRATOR.)

NARRATOR. Meanwhile, the Bottler is on the move, with Miss Simmons and Mister Fleagle, and they stop by the roadside, and Miss Simmons says—

MISS SIMMONS: Uh oh. The Bottler's thinking.

NARRATOR: And the Bottler says—

BOTTLER: Why "Uh oh"?

MISS SIMMONS: Thinking's O K.

NARRATOR: —says Miss Simmons.

MISS SIMMONS: But I'd rather do sex, play the piano, or kill someone than stand here and watch you think.

FLEAGLE: Yeah.

MISS SIMMONS: Watching you think is boring...

(A fortune teller appears, who is the same LITTLE PERSON *we've met before. This time, the* LITTLE PERSON *has a long speaking trumpet to talk to the fortunee, so that no one else can hear the inquirer's fate. The teller stands on a box, and a lantern hangs off a tree branch nearby.)*

LITTLE PERSON: The future revealed! Ten cents.

MISS SIMMONS: I want my fortune told. Fleagle, you got a dime?

FLEAGLE: Ask the Bottler.

MISS SIMMONS: You got a dime?

BOTTLER: *(To fortune teller)* We'll pay after the fortune.

LITTLE PERSON: *(To* BOTTLER.*)* What happened to your face?

BOTTLER: Skip the insults. Fortune first, or Mister Fleagle will turn out your light.

LITTLE PERSON: O K, already.

(The LITTLE PERSON *speaks into* MISS SIMMONS' *ear with the trumpet. The* BOTTLER *and* FLEAGLE *attempt to overhear.* MISS SIMMONS *is shaken by whatever she's hearing. She starts to cry. The* BOTTLER *grabs the speaking trumpet and pulls it away from her ear.)*

BOTTLER: We got business. Let's get out of here.

LITTLE PERSON: Ten cents.

BOTTLER: Fish for it.

(They begin to exit, but the fortune teller calls after the BOTTLER.*)*

LITTLE PERSON: I'll tell your future for free. Your dream will come to nothing. Crows will tear your eyes out, and you'll go blind and silent into old age, alone and without the strength to kill yourself.

BOTTLER: You don't frighten me. Let's go.

(*This scene fades, as we return to the* DOCTOR'S *office. As he works on* YOUNG SAM, OLD SAM *appears behind them.*)

OLD SAM: Doctors are liars and thieves. The body screams for help, and they give it a shot and say goodnight. Last time the nurse is sitting at my bed, blonde, and she holds my hand and talks to me… and then someone says "Give him his shot.… Lots of others on the ward, honey. Give him a shot and say goodnight…" (*He is gone.*)

NARRATOR: (AUTHOR) The doc has a pharmacist's degree from a correspondence school in Pittsburgh, Pennsylvania. But after his third conviction, no one would let him stand behind the counter. He could not find a wheel to turn. One night he sucked up a little juice and thought it over at a place called Ernesto's near Three Rivers stadium. The answer came to him. He moved to Mexico, right below the border.

DOCTOR: (*Finishing with* YOUNG SAM.) Good as new. You're healed. (*He reaches into a box, takes out an amulet on a chain.*) Want one?

NARRATOR: (AUTHOR) The doctor is holding a little amulet, actually a rose colored cameo of the doctor himself in profile, with the words "Believe in me" inscribed on the back in a florid hand. (*He is gone.*)

DOCTOR: It's free. Helps keep the faith.

YOUNG SAM: No, thanks. But perhaps you'd be interested in a few choice…Ah, the hell with it. You did a good job. How come you're down here…

DOCTOR: *(Sings)* "South of the border, down Mexico way—that's where I fell in love, the stars above..." I prefer it.

YOUNG SAM: You hiding from someone?

(The DOCTOR laughs.)

DOCTOR: That's what all my patients say...except one. Years ago. You remind me of him.

YOUNG SAM: Yeah. Who?

DOCTOR: Lila's brother. He was here for awhile, after I patched him up. Brilliant man. Quite the chemist. We distilled a few powerful psychic energizers from some interesting local flora. By prescription only, of course.

YOUNG SAM: When he left, did he say where he was going?

DOCTOR: No, but he did leave this map.

(The DOCTOR takes a map out of his pocket, hands it to YOUNG SAM. Lights fade, and up on LILA, in her travelling clothes.)

LILA: Can't trust men to do damn all. Ten. Ten fiances in the last three years. I sent all of them to find what's mine. None of them ever came back. I had a feeling about Sam, though. He was the dumbest—or maybe he just loved me the most, and I thought maybe he'd stumble through to the end, where all those other guys just...I don't know what happened to them. Maybe they got lost. Maybe they met the Bottler. Maybe they failed, and were too ashamed to come back. Maybe once they got there, they forgot all about Lila... Now I'm going wherever it is I sent everyone else. Sometimes when I look in the mirror, my face frightens me. There's some need I don't understand right below the skin, that wants to tear through. Sometimes it feels like as long as I'm flesh and bone, I'll never rest. That's not

true. I'll end it, and then I'll rest—one way or another.
(She exits.)

10

(A NARRATOR *appears, holding a putter.)*

NARRATOR: At the miniature golf course, Scene 10.

(The NARRATOR *goes off as* YOUNG SAM *enters.)*

YOUNG SAM: Lila's brother marked out a route—and
I'm following his faded pencil line. So this map is a tool
to figure where I am in relation to something a helluva
lot bigger than me. Kind of religious, don't you think?

(In a wooden booth, the MANAGER *of the golf course
appears, reading a large book. He has a row of golf clubs
and balls. Over the booth, a sign with a painting of the solar
system and the words: Solar System Miniature Golf—Eight
Holes Only.* YOUNG SAM *approaches.)*

MANAGER: Get outta my light.

YOUNG SAM: Uh, I'm quite the reader myself. Looks
like an old book you got there.

MANAGER: Old? It's new as tomorrow. This is…"Secret
Councils of a Certain Exile." Among other tidbits, it
includes the architect's complete plans for the tower of
Babel.

YOUNG SAM: That's very interesting. You know, I happen to have with me a number of books, including
one you may have heard of—Hiram Birdseed at the
World's Fair. *(Aside to audience)* This Hiram Birdseed at
the World's Fair is my biggest seller. These books are
all published by the same company in Philadelphia.
For men only, you know the kind…

MANAGER: Not interested. I already have this excellent
book.

YOUNG SAM: How do you know? You barely started it.

MANAGER: I wrote it. Are you playing? Or looking for Lila's brother?

YOUNG SAM: I…

MANAGER: Why didn't you say so? He helped me build this place. Every hole a different planet. In fact, it was his idea to have only eight holes. "Leave out the earth," he says. "Too dull."

NARRATOR: A gentleman with eight flags.

MANAGER: I used to have another miniature golf course. Earth only. Had a first hole called Constantinople. The ball needed to go through the door of the palace of the Imam, then between the Bosphorous and the Hellespont. Second hole was a bridge at Florence, the ball rolled among carriages and men on horseback crossing over in both directions. Underneath, an aquatic expedition set out on the Arno. Third hole had a…

YOUNG SAM: About Lila's…

MANAGER: I know exactly where he is. (*He hands Young Sam a club.*) Play a round.

YOUNG SAM: I don't play golf.

(*The MANAGER picks up another club, leaps out of his booth, and fences with YOUNG SAM, until YOUNG SAM is backed into a corner, the club poised over his head.*)

MANAGER: Golf? What has all this to do with golf? You want to know, don't you? Get on the course.

YOUNG SAM: O K, O K. (*He takes his club, heads for the course.*)

MANAGER: Start with Hole One, Mercury. The one that looks like a cracked landscape of ice.

YOUNG SAM: I thought Mercury was hot.

MANAGER: Not in my brain, it isn't. When you finish, I'll have a surprise for you.

(The company, as other miniature golf customers, enter.)

MANAGER: Ah, more truth seekers.

(YOUNG SAM exits to begin play. The company golfs. CAPABILITY BROWN enters with a vine covered putter. As be speaks, OLD SAM, the BOTTLER, MISS SIMMONS, and FLEAGLE [caddying], LILA, and the company members play different holes.)

NARRATOR: A GARDEN INTERLUDE, with Mister Capability Brown.

CAPABILITY BROWN: THE RULES FOR THE CREATION OF ELYSIUM IN THE ENGLISH COUNTRYSIDE. A Paradise for all seasons.

NARRATOR: WINTER.

CAPABILITY BROWN: The evergreens: holly, ivy and the well attired woodbine. Juniper for gin.

NARRATOR: SPRING.

CAPABILITY BROWN: Violets, daffadillies, sweet briar, peonies and honeysuckle.

NARRATOR: SUMMER.

CAPABILITY BROWN: Columbine, apricocks, wild vine and laurel.

NARRATOR: FALL.

CAPABILITY BROWN: The apple, poppies, pumpkins, and all melons come to fruit. Have the following: in the earth: Mounds, grottos, crypts. On the earth: groves, labyrinths, fountains. In the air: aviaries containing the ostrich, peacocks, swans, and cranes. Buzzy bees. A slew of automata among the rocks. Include my patented mechanism for the production of artificial echoes.

NARRATOR: Echoes.

CAPABILITY BROWN: Statuary as follows: Voluptia, goddess of pleasure; Sylvanus, god of the woods; and Agerona, goddess of silence. Areas should be set aside for a medical garden, a spiritual garden, and for garden burial. This garden should be so linked to nature that a man could stumble in without realizing he is in a garden at all. In fact...

NARRATOR: END OF GARDEN INTERLUDE.

(OLD SAM *enters with putter, playing as* CAPABILITY BROWN *moves on.*)

OLD SAM: *(Calling after* CAPABILITY BROWN*)* Dollar a hole? *(To audience)* I'm too old to waste time being clever. All this really happened, and nothing is changed to amuse you. This is not some story I've told myself so often that I believe it. It's true as death. Come the end, it's over and it don't play back. Unlike life, death doesn't happen in your mind. It's a cool clear note from outside, high and sharp enough to break the shell.

(*A* WOMAN *approaches* OLD SAM. *She's holding a 46 Pontiac carburetor, and a putter.*)

WOMAN: Last night, I was playing through, 3 A M, they landed right there on the seventh. Neptune. Took me right inside the ship. This big one says "I, the advance scout of the invasion force, have proven we are invincible. Is it not better to live as our slaves, rather than be exterminated?" What could I say? Let them know back in Pittsburgh. They said we were living wrong here on earth. "Stop all that stupid shit," they said. They gave me this signalling device, if I ever want to contact them!

OLD SAM: That's a '46 Pontiac carburetor.

WOMAN: Is it now?

(As OLD SAM *leaves, the* WOMAN *turns to audience.)*

WOMAN: Let 'em know back in Pittsburgh!

*(*WOMAN *exits, and the* BOTTLER, FLEAGLE *and* MISS SIMMONS *enter.* FLEAGLE *carries the* BOTTLER's *putter. As they play…)*

BOTTLER: Its 3 A M at Chez Bottler. Down a hallway carpeted in Astroturf…

MISS SIMMONS: Shade?

BOTTLER: Crimson—a clown with an enormous pair of shears skips toward room 33. On the roof of Chez Bottler the anti-aircraft guns swivel slowly on their turrets, fingers of light probe the sky…

*(*FLEAGLE *hands the* BOTTLER *the putter. The* BOTTLER *putts. All look.)*

FLEAGLE: Nice shot!

BOTTLER: Wasn't it. We're close. I can feel it. Next stop…next stop and we'll have him.

(The BOTTLER *and his crew exit.* YOUNG SAM *plays the last hole, and the* MANAGER *comes out to greet him.)*

MANAGER: You played through.

YOUNG SAM: Yeah.

MANAGER: Did you…get it?

YOUNG SAM: Get what?

MANAGER: Never mind. Note my eyes.

YOUNG SAM: Very light colored. Almost white.

NARRATOR: Very light eyes.

MANAGER: They were always light, but now—exceptionally. The powerful use of the brain makes the eyes lighter. What color are yours?

YOUNG SAM: Brown.

MANAGER: Of course. *(He embraces* YOUNG SAM.*)* You found me at last! I am Lila's brother! Got any gum?

YOUNG SAM: What kind do you want?

MANAGER: Doublemint.

YOUNG SAM: I've only got exploding gum.

MANAGER: Well, tell me all about Lila. How'd you know where to find me? What'd she tell you about the money?

YOUNG SAM: Bullshit. You're not her brother. You're not the missing man. You try to find someone, you get to know him…

MANAGER: If I'm not Lila's brother, how would I know all these details? You saw the man with the light? Didn't you? I smoke Luckies, don't I?

YOUNG SAM: Somebody told you that stuff. I'm leaving. Here's your golf club.

MANAGER: Damn right somebody told me. All Lila's other "fiances" who've been coming this way for ten years.

YOUNG SAM: You're lying. You gotta be.

MANAGER: Deadheads and suckers. Nobody finds him, or that money. Leave, why don't you. I'm gonna play a round. *(Picks up putter)* Don't think that if you find him, he'll have more to show you than this! Fore!

(The MANAGER *is gone. The* LITTLE PERSON *in the dirty yellow vest appears. She is carrying a box with holes in the top.)*

LITTLE PERSON: Got a butt?

YOUNG SAM: It's you again. Who are you?

LITTLE PERSON: I'm nobody. Who are you?

YOUNG SAM: My Uncle Sam. Hey…

LITTLE PERSON: Just kidding…I'm in show business. Show's in here. *(Holds up box)* Rats. I run a rat theater. But the show's not in A-1 shape. Yesterday, we were doing a matinee of Romeo and Juliet when a dog broke into the show tent and ate the cast. These are only the understudies.

YOUNG SAM: You been following me.

LITTLE PERSON: Or vice-versa. I'll put my cards on the table. In fact, I'll put my cards on the floor. You got troubles ahead. Go to the church of Saint Christopher. Watch out for Lila.

YOUNG SAM: Lila?

LITTLE PERSON: Then go to the Blowhole Theatre. Gotta run. There's the travel agent.

YOUNG SAM: Hey—wait…

(The TRAVEL AGENT appears, with his female assistant as the LITTLE PERSON runs off.)

TRAVEL AGENT. Hey! How you been? Where to this time? You know, from the looks of you, you got quite a streak of bad luck going.

WOMAN: HA HA HA.

TRAVEL AGENT. Mister, you must have done something real bad in this life to get paid off that way. Or in some other life. You ever consider…

YOUNG SAM: I wanna make some travel arrangements.

TRAVEL AGENT. So it's like that, is it? Passport!

YOUNG SAM: Uh…I didn't think I needed…

TRAVEL AGENT. The little book, sir. The one that tells you who you are.

YOUNG SAM: I know who I am.

TRAVEL AGENT. Do you now?

WOMAN: HA HA HA.

TRAVEL AGENT. Purpose of travel? Business? Or pleasure?

(YOUNG SAM *takes out some money, holds it up. The* TRAVEL AGENT *takes it.*)

TRAVEL AGENT. Where did you say, sir?

YOUNG SAM: The Church of Saint Christopher.

TRAVEL AGENT. Wonderful choice, sir. My most popular destination this year.

YOUNG SAM: Where is this church exactly?

TRAVEL AGENT. In the city of Pittsburgh, state of Pennsylvania, land of enchantment.

YOUNG SAM: You're kidding.

TRAVEL AGENT. Sir, you'll love it. Pittsburgh is noted for its wonderful humidity. On the average night, you can take an easy chair out on the tarantula, and relax in the cool breeze.

WOMAN: HA HA HA.

TRAVEL AGENT. Majestic mountains, sparkling rivers, breathtaking buildings, gorgeous gardens. The scenery's nice too.

WOMAN: HA HA HA.

YOUNG SAM: I can't believe this.

TRAVEL AGENT. Your tickets.

YOUNG SAM: Thanks.

TRAVEL AGENT. You'll love the boat ride. Ocean all the way.

WOMAN: HA HA HA.

YOUNG SAM: There's no water between…

TRAVEL AGENT. And remember our motto: Everywhere you go, there you are! *(He is gone.)*

NARRATOR: While in transit, My Uncle Sam studies his final lesson from the Universal Detective Agency.

YOUNG SAM: Here goes.

(The following "cassette," as usual, is performed by the company on mike around YOUNG SAM.*)*

CASSETTE: GETTING YOUR MAN: Be sure you've got the right party. Remember: people can change, and not just their height, weight, sex, and facial structure... even the nature of the twinkle in their eye. The cub detective can easily drop into the chief pitfall in the search for Missing Persons. Philosophy. If you find yourself beginning to search for its own sake, or thinking of your search as a quest of some sacred kind, or feeling that the search itself is the goal and whether you find the missing man or not is simply a question of plot: THESE ARE DANGER SIGNS. STOP! Remember the client! And most vital of all—if you find yourself not calling in to the office, not seeing your friends, getting a divorce, telling your girlfriend you won't be seeing her for awhile...if you have a strange attraction for anonymous hotels on sidestreets, faceless coffee shops. If you lose the ability to tell one city from another. If you see a sign that says "transients only" and you say "home sweet home" ...you yourself are becoming missing...and the Universal Detective Agency will have to send a student out to find you. That's a joke—but being missing is not funny. *(Raucous laughter)*

11

(The Church of Saint Christopher. Appropriate music and prayers)

NARRATOR: At last My Uncle Sam arrives to pay a pious visit to the Church of Saint Christopher— and to ask a few questions. He arrives at the sanctuary—late.

PENITENTS: *Mea culpa, mea culpa, mea culpa. In nomine Patri, Filii, et Spiritu Sanctu... (Repeats)*

(A SACRISTAN *approaches* YOUNG SAM.*)*

SACRISTAN: I'm sorry to tell you that the Holy Crows have already gone piously to roost. These are not the original Holy Crows, of course, but their descendents...the grandchildren of the very Holy Crows that tore out the eyes of the murderers of Saint Christopher. However, I could officially arouse them for a small fee. Ten cents.

NARRATOR: Sam was broke, and besides...

YOUNG SAM: I'm not interested in any crows. I'm looking for a guy called Lila's brother. Do you know anything about...

SACRISTAN: I believe you will find what the Holy Crows have to say on the subject to be not devoid of interest.

YOUNG SAM: The crows?

SACRISTAN: Ten cents.

NARRATOR: Sam was broke. He hadda unload something on this holy father.

YOUNG SAM: Uh...father, I got here a French ring, with a view. The ring is genuine imitation platinum, and set in the top here is your choice of picture. Bathing Beauties! ...Uh... Views of the Panama Canal? How about the luminous crucifix?

(YOUNG SAM *shows it. The* SACRISTAN *stares at it.*)

SACRISTAN: You are out of your mind. The insane are God's special children. For you, I'll wake the crows for nothing. Follow me.

NARRATOR: The sacristan led My Uncle Sam toward the far end of the cloister, where there sat two curious birds.

(*The* HOLY CROWS *are revealed on their perch. They are two gigantic black crows, with bright yellow beaks.*)

SACRISTAN: These birds, by the holy mathematics of the silver wires and instruments winded among their entrails, and on into their small throats, freely whistle their natural field notes.

(*The* CROWS *are silent. The* SACRISTAN *pokes them with a stick.*)

CROWS: Caw! Caw! Caw!

SACRISTAN: They are able to move with natural grace in all their parts. But so closely beneath the feathers are all these instruments obscured, that the pious renounce conjectures of art, and say it is done by God's grace. The cause of many conversions. Pressure on this stone in the floor sets them in motion.

YOUNG SAM: They're fakes.

SACRISTAN: Of course. I built them myself, with God's guidance.

YOUNG SAM: But they couldn't fool anyone. Too big. Everyone knows…

SACRISTAN: All the holy secrets are what everyone knows. Obvious. God is love, yes? All flesh is grass. The wages of sin is death.

NARRATOR: In the back pew, three worshippers. Their expressions were pure and holy—almost tragic. In fact, the trio were overdoing it a bit even for the Church

of Saint Christopher. They looked like they were
discussing the medical expenses of a dying patient...

(YOUNG SAM *spots the* BOTTLER, FLEAGLE *and* MISS
SIMMONS. *They spot him, rush toward him.*)

YOUNG SAM: I think I'm in some trouble here, father.

SACRISTAN: What trouble, my son? Does God not exist?
Are we not men?

FLEAGLE: *(Screaming)* You were warned!

(The SACRISTAN, *behind Young Sam's back, slips away.*)

BOTTLER: What, may I ask, are you doing here?

YOUNG SAM: I'm uh...security man for the church,
guarding the crows. Ask the Sacristan.

MISS SIMMONS: What Sacristan? There's no one here
but us.

FLEAGLE: We warned you to change your act, or go
back to the woods.

BOTTLER: That money's mine. I'm meeting the missing
man first, and only. But you'll go further than anyone
who's just disappeared. Much further. I'm going to
have Mister Fleagle and Miss Simmons—

*(*FLEAGLE *grabs* YOUNG SAM, *takes him down to his knees,
holds him helpless.*)

BOTTLER: —administer to you a tremendous overdose
of a certain drug that will cause you to forget who
you are. *(He hands a hypodermic to* MISS SIMMONS.*)*
Permanently. Then we'll leave you to wander off about
the world. Simpler than killing. A corpse is dirty.
You'll be listed as missing. A missing person is as
transparent as glass. Nothing left to clean up or throw
away.
I have a dream. Gently, Fleagle...soon. No one can be
allowed to interfere with the creation of Chez Bottler!
As you are still disturbed by these impossible fantasies

of finding someone, when you can't even find yourself, the sooner you lose your mind entirely the better. Perhaps some charitable institution will provide you with a dark room and clean straw, where you can dream forever of Lila, and her brother, and the Bottler. Now, Miss Simmons. Now!

(As the BOTTLER *says this, he steps beneath the* CROWS, *stepping on the stone that activates them. They writhe forward off their perch, attacking the* BOTTLER.*)*

CROWS: Caw! Caw! Caw!

*(*CROWS *peck out his eyes. Blood streams from between the* BOTTLER'*s fingers as he holds his face. He's in agony. The* CROWS *return to their perch.* FLEAGLE *and* MISS SIMMONS *stare, letting* YOUNG SAM *go. The* SACRISTAN *enters,* LILA *behind him.)*

SACRISTAN: The principal virtue of these marvelous crows, beyond their efficacy in conversion, is that they have no practical use. Like music, they are solely for the recreation of the mind.

(The BOTTLER *staggers off, blind and in pain.* FLEAGLE *and* MISS SIMMONS *follow. Before she exits,* MISS SIMMONS *turns back.)*

MISS SIMMONS: You never understood him, any of you! *(She exits.)*

YOUNG SAM: Lila! You're here!

SACRISTAN: Lila's brother is close. Nearby. Go through the Blowhole Theatre.

*(*YOUNG SAM *heads toward* LILA *and the church entrance.)*

SACRISTAN: Those doors are locked for the night. You can't go back the way you came.

(The LITTLE PERSON *in the dirty yellow vest emerges from behind the* CROWS.*)*

LITTLE PERSON: Follow me.

12

(The LITTLE PERSON *leads* LILA *and* YOUNG SAM *away.
The cloister is gone, and the Blowhole Theatre appears.*
LILA, LITTLE PERSON *and* YOUNG SAM *reappear at one
side of this "theatre". At the rear of the Blowhole Theatre set
is a multicolored house exterior, with a lunatic's grinning
face painted on the door. A tree stands in this house's very
green front yard. Hot dogs grow on its branches. There's
a large pink doghouse. A seascape is in the distance, with
moving waves. In front of it all, a low white picket fence,
with flowers. On the side of the set furthest from* LILA *and*
YOUNG SAM *there is a large sign reading EXIT—with an
arrow, pointing to the only way out. This exit sign is at the
base of a large papier-mâché elephant, crimson tusks with
yellow tips. A man is in a howdah on the elephant's back
with his hands on control levers. A* FARMER *[overalls, corn-
cob pipe] peering through a telescope and holding a cattle
prod, is onstage along with a rather sinister-looking Clown,
and other Blowhole Theatre personnel.)*

*(Note: The set suggested here for the Blowhole Theatre is one
idea. In any case, a garish American sideshow.)*

NARRATOR: The Blowhole Theatre— A passageway!
Scene 42.

(A PITCHMAN *enters. Music, loud, as the Blowhole
personnel and set come alive. The* PITCHMAN *holds a
Viewmaster.)*

PITCHMAN: YOWZAA! YOWZAA! YOWZAA! The
world famous BLOWHOLE THEATRE has got it all!
This show is all meat and no potatoes. Remember,
ladies and gentlemen, that the cool of the evening is the
perfect time to see the BLOWHOLE THEATRE, and to
mark its many pee-cool-i-arities! Pay at the door. No
tickee. No washee. *(To self)* People want blood for ten
cents.

(ANOTHER PITCHMAN *enters, with a large scale.)*

ANOTHER PITCHMAN. Not a show you go to! A show you go through! Guess your weight, occupation or age! Winna prize! Just one thin dime, the tenth part of a dollar. Guess your age! *(To the* LITTLE PERSON*)* Hell, I'll even guess your sex!

*(*LILA *grabs* YOUNG SAM*'s hand, pulling him toward the Blowhole stage.)*

LILA: Sam, let's go. We're so close.

*(*YOUNG SAM *stops* LILA*.)*

YOUNG SAM: You sent a lot of other men on this crazy search, didn't you, Lila? Did you promise to marry them too?

LILA: I'm sorry, Sam. I lied to you. I wanted what was mine, and it was the only way I had…I was hoping you'd be the one. *(Beat)* I was. That's the truth.

LITTLE PERSON: Leave him alone. She knew you could be killed.

YOUNG SAM: Did you think the Bottler would kill me, Lila? Did you care about that when you sent me for your money? Or maybe I'd kill him? Or we'd find it and kill each other, and both be out of your way.

LILA: Sam, I knew something bad might happen— but I didn't want it to—

LITTLE PERSON: Lila, go home. *(She takes off her hat, and the rest of her disguise. She is a young woman, now in a dress, with long hair.)*

LILA: Darlene…?

YOUNG SAM: You're Darlene? Lila's brother's wife?

DARLENE: There's no money anymore, Lila. He spent it all long ago, and he doesn't want to see you.

LILA: Bastard. Both of you bastards. Is that true? What did he do with all that money?

DARLENE: He made a garden.

(The exit sign of the Blowhole Theatre revolves, revealing the words TO THE GARDEN.)

NARRATOR: Last Garden Interlude.

(CAPABILITY BROWN appears.)

CAPABILITY BROWN: Gardens are maps of paradise, but tricky ones. Certain gardens are dependent for their effect on being viewed in a certain order, like words on a page. Some gardens are puzzles, and demand solutions. Others have made their most beautiful areas impossible to reach, like a goal in a dream. And there are gardens that lead us to believe we've been all through them, and then we realize we've only been in a small corner, a simple temple or grove. Outside, the entire garden awaits us still. Our true life, the spirit in everything—is invisible. Yet it moves men, and beasts, rivers and trees, and in their movements, we can learn to see it, even in a single leaf, in the blink of an eye. On these nearby grounds lives a hermit. He built all this: the Opium Den, this Blowhole Theatre, the lighthouse, the nightclub in Pittsburgh, and the pleasant walks and groves between. Then he made himself a simple cottage, with an herb garden. He then built a place yet simpler, a kind of hut. Now he lives by a stick he has stuck into the ground, and he's hung from it a water gourd. I think he may soon move again... Perhaps I'll write a garden book. I have no doubt I would produce, a volume of uncommon use, that will be worthy to be placed, beneath the eye of men of taste. What man of taste my right will doubt to put things in—or leave them out. Perhaps I'd do better to live in a tree—sleep my days away on a sofa of goosefoot vine.

LILA: *(To* DARLENE *and* YOUNG SAM*)* It looks like I'm not wanted here.

YOUNG SAM: Did you ever love me, Lila?

LILA: I don't know. Maybe I did and I didn't know it. Sam, I'm leaving. There's nothing for me here. Come back with me...please. This time, no promises. You wouldn't believe them anyway.

DARLENE: You're a liar, Lila. You're scared and lonely now, so you'll beg him to hold your hand. He's much too good for you.

LILA: You coming, Sam?

(A long beat)

YOUNG SAM: No, Lila. I'll stay.

*(*LILA *exits.* YOUNG SAM *looks after her. To* DARLENE*)*

YOUNG SAM: That was wrong. You shouldn't have done that. *(Long beat. To himself)* I shouldn't have done that.

*(*YOUNG SAM *hesitantly starts off after* LILA*, but Darlene stops him.)*

DARLENE: You want to meet him, don't you? You want to see the garden, don't you? This is the only way to go!

*(*DARLENE *pulls* YOUNG SAM *down with her onto the stage of the Blowhole Theatre. Music. The* FARMER *and the* CLOWN *leap into action. The* CLOWN *blocks their way. The* FARMER *pulls down a window shade from a tree limb. On it is a painting of the sun and moon. The elephant's eyes light up red. Other Blowhole Theatre performers dance.)*

CLOWN: Do you do the cakewalk? Sarabande?

FARMER: Black Bottom? Gavotte?

*(*FARMER *uses his cattle prod to make* DARLENE *and* YOUNG SAM *dance.)*

CLOWN: *(Dancing)* Have you trod the quaint mazes in the wanton green? Done the hokey pokey?

(The music ends abruptly. The FARMER *grabs* YOUNG SAM'*s face and appeals to the* HOWDAH MAN, *who is suddenly wearing a white wig. A trial.)*

FARMER/ATTORNEY: Look at the face of my client! Is this the face of a guilty man? An undeserving man? A man who shouldn't receive his perfect birthright!

(The HOWDAH MAN/JUDGE *growls and snarls.)*

FARMER/ATTORNEY: These allegations are false! I demand to cross examine the alligator! *(He turns to* DARLENE.) You his accomplice?

DARLENE: I just helped him to…

CLOWN, FARMER & PITCHMEN: We thought so!

*(*HOWDAH MAN/JUDGE *growls again.)*

FARMER/ATTORNEY: *(Stage whisper)* Sam, it's hopeless. Your case won't hold water. *(He rubs his fingers together—the gesture for money. He winks.)*

YOUNG SAM: I'm broke.

*(*DARLENE *hands* YOUNG SAM *a dime.)*

YOUNG SAM: I've got ten cents. *(He hands it to* FARMER.*)* Will this plug the leak?

FARMER/ATTORNEY: This'll not only plug it, it'll water-proof it at the same time.

*(*FARMER *hands the dime to the* CLOWN, *who hands it up to the* HOWDAH MAN/JUDGE.*)*

HOWDAH MAN/JUDGE: Let me rebalance the scales of justice…

CLOWN: If he can't rebalance it, I knows a man, who knows a man, who can rebalance it…

FARMER & CLOWN. Shhh!

HOWDAH MAN/JUDGE: Innocent!

CLOWN: Innocent!

FARMER/ATTORNEY: Innocent!

PITCHMAN: Innocent?

HOWDAH MAN/JUDGE: Head for the exit!

DARLENE: Let's go.

(Music. The floor wiggles, tossing them to the ground. The CLOWN leaps about hysterically. A blast of air blows DARLENE's dress up above her waist. Other Blowhole personnel dance. Faces of other characters appear grinning in the house's windows. DARLENE grabs YOUNG SAM's hand.)

FARMER/ATTORNEY: *(Shouting.)* Keep moving! Give all of youself away!

(They bolt through the exit. They're gone, and so is the Blowhole Theatre set. The Blowhole Theatre actors place themselves in a straggly line, except one, who gawks at the others.)

NARRATOR: In its infancy, the Blowhole Theatre Company once performed an adaptation of Hiram Birdseed at the World's Fair. It consisted of mindless gawking by one member of the company, while the others paraded by dressed as all the people of the earth. *(They do so, and exit.)*

13

(The garden. The stage is almost bare, green. DARLENE and YOUNG SAM. OLD SAM, alone, toward the rear.)

NARRATOR: In the garden.

OLD SAM: He's not doing so badly. I even like him. He's doing his very very best. You know, you get on,

and you cross over somehow. I can feel in my mind my
entire life there for me—all at once. Confusing after so
many years of being stuck in time. Floating between
gears—I'm here and I'm in the garden. It's no choice.
It's all together. I don't need to make those choices
anymore.

DARLENE: *(To* YOUNG SAM*)* You've come a long way.
My husband disappeared to lose himself, to hide from
everything he was, The money helped. He built a place
to forget himself in, to make someone new. *(Laughing)*
He doesn't even remember his name.

YOUNG SAM: Does he know you?

DARLENE: *(Laughs)* There are things he hasn't forgotten.

YOUNG SAM: Why did you help me get here?

DARLENE: We wanted company. Someone to help us.
The garden needs care. Wait here. I'll bring him. The
truth is that this world is paradise. If you don't believe
me, look around.

*(*DARLENE *exits.* OLD SAM *and* YOUNG SAM *onstage,* OLD
SAM *at some distance behind* YOUNG SAM*. The* AUTHOR
enters.)

AUTHOR. And he did. And it seemed to My Uncle
Sam that everything was there for his sake, and that
everything spoke to him. The flowers nodded in
greeting, the clouds above foretold great wonders, and
the statues smiled their enigmatic smiles. He was sure
beyond any doubt that an urgent meaning was there—
but he couldn't read it—not so he could tell it back to
you. That it was there was enough. *(The Author is gone.)*

YOUNG SAM: I saw the river flowing through the
garden, and on either side of the river, trees bearing
all manner of fruit, and the fruit of the trees were for
the healing of nations…*(He takes a few steps toward the
audience.)* At this moment, it doesn't seem, after all the

way I've come, that there's any stopping place. Seems
to me I go from one place to another in the blink of an
eye... Even this garden's only one step...seeing it all
from over my head somewhere...

OLD SAM & YOUNG SAM: ...like a gull, wandering
between heaven and earth and looking down, all so
easy. I'm floating out everywhere and turning like the
rolling earth itself in this travelling of mine...I can be
everywhere, and the world—the world just can't help
itself in some beautiful way...

YOUNG SAM: And I saw all this in the garden, and my
own life jumped up at me like a puppy inside. (*Long
beat.*)

OLD SAM: I didn't stay.

(*YOUNG SAM exits. OLD SAM's hotel room returns, and he
goes to it, sits in his chair. In the distance, the singing duo.
This time they actually sing, no lip sync, and no music.*)

DUO.
This is my story, I have no song
Just a lone and broken heart,
Just because I fell in love, in love with you
I pray, that you'll come back to me
Just to hear you say you love me
And we'll never, never part...
(*They fade, and are gone.*)

14

OLD SAM: Sioux city sue...soo city soo...her hair is
blonde her eye is blue...swap my horse and dog
for you...Lila was gone when I got back. I asked
everybody, searched everywhere. Nothing. She was
gone, that's all. Disappeared... Soo city soo...I used
to want my own place to live, where I could just die
without inconveniencing anyone. Now I don't mind

that the maid'll scream when she finds my body.
White frost covers the garden. The flowers freeze in
the night, wake up before dawn as white ghosts of
themselves, shapes alone, with no life left. All one
whiteness in the pre-dawn dark, and then the morning
sun rises and melts the frost, and it flows down into
the roots, and gives us life. Ice and water. Same stuff.
A pine cone drops in the winter garden. Frost on the
chrysanthemums. Lila's dead now. I see her, and
she's laughing, and her memory draws me toward
the grave. Who says that the dead don't think of us?
Lila thinks of me all the time… This morning I woke
suddenly, and wasn't sure where I was…like a gull,
lost between heaven and earth… Downstairs, there's a
woman, got two kids and a black eye, moved in three
weeks ago, running away from some man. I believe the
Child Services pays her bills. He hasn't found her yet,
and she's looking better. Not so scared. This morning
she says "Hello My Uncle Sam" in the coffee shop.
Tonight those two kids of hers can't sleep. They feel
I'm gonna die. So they sit up in bed, eyes wide open,
waiting. Their momma comes in and says, "You got
school tomorrow, go to sleep," and they say "we can't
sleep momma, something's gonna happen… *(He holds
his chest in pain.)* No doctor. Don't call a doctor. I don't
need no doctor. It's all right. If you don't know it, it's
a two lane road, and I'm coming back the other way. I
got a return ticket. See you all again sometime…

(Lights dim on OLD SAM, *as* YOUNG SAM *appears.)*

YOUNG SAM: I am my Uncle Sam. What can't be said,
can't be said, and it can't be whistled either…

*(*YOUNG SAM *strolls off, whistling, past* OLD SAM, *who is
very still. The* AUTHOR *appears.)*

AUTHOR: There's My Uncle Sam…sitting alone in his
hotel room in Pittsburgh…Sherman Arms. There's his

cashmere coat, and his cigar in the ashtray. He's got
the sweetest expression on his face ... I got a nephew,
name's Jesse. He sees me every now and then, and I
say "How you doin', Jess'," and we go down to the
video arcade, and I lay five bucks worth of quarters
on him. He sees me all right, with my cashmere coat
and my cigar. Corona Corona, get 'em five for a dollar,
cigar stand, Sherman Arms. Come dusk, last sun
through the lace curtains, and I sit in a leather armchair
in the lobby. I am My Uncle Sam.
Statues of My Uncle Sam across America! Winter,
and there's snow on his shoulders, and a little perfect
mound of snow sits in the crown of his hat where no
one can see it but the birds. In the summer, someone
wreathes the brow of the statue with flowers.

END OF PLAY

NOTE ON SONGS AND RECORDINGS

For performances of copyrighted songs or recordings used in this play, the permission of the copyright owner(s) must be obtained. Other songs or recordings may be substituted provided permission from the copyright owner(s) of such songs, arrangements or recordings is obtained; or songs or recordings in the public domain may be substituted.

p1, p73: *This Is My Story,* Gene and Eunice
p7-8: *Cross Over the Bridge,* Flamingos
p19, 24-25: *Wheel of Fortune,* Kay Starr
p27: *Who's Honey Are You,* Ruth Etting
p73: *Sioux City Sue,* Gene Autry